LIVE FIRE BBQ AND BEYOND

Recipes for Outdoor Cooking with
Your Kamado, Pizza Oven,
Fire Pit, Rotisserie and More

WENDY O'NEAL

Ulysses Press

Published by:
Ulysses Press
P.O. Box 3440
Berkeley, CA 94703
www.ulyssespress.com

ISBN: 978-1-61243-899-3
Library of Congress Catalog Number: 2018967978

Printed in Canada by Marquis Book Printing
10 9 8 7 6 5 4 3 2 1

Acquisitions editor: Bridget Thoreson
Managing editor: Claire Chun
Project editor: Molly Conway
Editor: Renee Rutledge
Proofreader: Lauren Harrison
Front cover design: Malea Clark-Nicholson
Cover photographs: back © Wendy O'Neal; front from shutterstock.com burger © Brent Hofacker, shrimp © Alieva Liubov, ribs © bitt24, pizza © Jag_cz, pineapple © Larisa Blinova, steak © Alexander Raths, charcoal background © NOPPHARAT STUDIO62
Interior design/layout: what!design @ whatweb.com
Interior photographs: © Wendy O'Neal except on pages 7, 11 (top), 81, 82, and 128 © Kate Eschbach; page 1 and chapter openers charcoal © NOPPHARAT STUDIO62/shutterstock.com; page 9 hearth cooking © Brownwyn Photo/shutterstock.com; page 15 chimney starter © Jari/shutterstock.com

Distributed by Publishers Group West

IMPORTANT NOTE TO READERS: This book is independently authored and published and no sponsorship or endorsement of this book by, and no affiliation with, any trademarked brands or products mentioned or pictured within is claimed or suggested. All trademarks that appear in this book belong to their respective owners and are used here for informational purposes only. The author and publisher encourage readers to patronize the quality brands and products pictured and mentioned in this book. Take special note of the important safety warnings throughout this book, and always use customary precautions for safe food preparation, handling, and storage.

To Kaylynn and Gavin. I am so blessed to have you call me mom!
Y'all are my everything.

And thanks for always eating your supper.

CONTENTS

INTRODUCTION

I grew up in a family that loved outdoor cooking. My dad was always firing up the grill for supper, lighting the smoker for weekend parties, and even teaching himself how to cook with the Dutch oven. When I married, my husband had no idea that we could make such delicious food at home. Sure, he'd had some of my dad's cooking, but most of his experience with barbecue or grilled foods came from chain restaurants.

Shortly after we were married, we bought an inexpensive grill and an outdoor cookbook, and we've been hooked on outdoor cooking ever since. We've had gas grills, charcoal grills, grills that only use newspaper, travel grills, tabletop grills—we've had them all. But my favorites are a good-quality kamado grill and my large gas grill.

I'm a self-taught cook, but I was given a great foundation in the kitchen by my mom and my granny. I remember watching cooking shows on PBS when I'd get home from school and writing down the recipes as the chefs cooked. I loved learning about new cuisines and discovering kitchen tips, so when the Food Network started, I was in heaven. I couldn't get enough! I had no desire to become a chef, I just wanted to be able to feed my family good food. The kitchen (and the backyard grill) is the heart of the home, where I love bringing family and friends together over a delicious meal.

LIVE FIRE COOKING

Live fire is the oldest way of cooking, and the fascination with live fire cooking is growing. There are restaurants that only cook with live fire; in fact, there is a local fast food joint that cooks everything with live fire on a gaucho grill, and it is delicious! Now, home cooks and backyard cooking enthusiasts are jumping on the bandwagon.

I use several methods of live fire cooking in my backyard. I have a kamado grill and a wood-fired pizza oven, but my favorite is just a little portable fire pit. It's simple and great for small, quick meals. Having friends and family sit around the little fire pit in my backyard while cooking a meal is priceless.

Live fire cooking doesn't take a lot of fancy ingredients or seasoning as the food is seared quickly, which gives it tons of flavor and caramelization. The moisture held in by the searing is released when you cut into the food just before serving. Also, the wood and/or lump charcoal impart flavor as well.

Live fire cooking is any type of cooking that uses fire as the heat source. Grills, wood-fired pizza ovens, fire pits, and hearths all use fire in some way. Whether you are using an active fire or smoldering wood or lump charcoal, it is live fire cooking. Many people have already tried live fire cooking when using a traditional grill or a fire while camping.

TYPES OF EQUIPMENT

Kamado Grills—A good kamado grill can do everything from live fire cooking and charcoal grilling to smoking and baking. Even delicious, crispy pizza is doable in a kamado. They really are a great, multipurpose piece of equipment to add to your backyard kitchen. There are several brands of kamado grills, such as Big Green Egg, Kamado Joe, and Char-Griller. My Char-Griller kamado grill works great and is a lot cheaper than some of the big-name brands.

Charcoal Grills—Charcoal grills come in a variety of sizes, but they all work the same. It's best to pick out one that has enough surface area to cook for your family. A chimney starter is useful in helping get a good fire going; however, most of the time the cooking will be done with hot coals instead of fire. The beginning of the cooking process can take place with the live fire, but as soon as the coals turn to ash they stop burning and remain hot for a long time. Longer grilling sessions require the addition of more charcoal to keep the grill hot.

Wood-Fired Pizza Ovens—Cooking in a wood-fired pizza oven is fun and produces a great flavor. There are a lot of brands on the market, but my favorite is from Forno Bravo (www.fornobravo .com). These ovens are an investment, so make sure to get a quality one that will fit everything you want to cook. I picked one that would be large enough to cook a whole turkey, a pan of lasagna, or enough pizza for my family all at once.

Fire Pits—Most of my experience with live fire cooking came from cooking over a fire pit while camping. There are no tricks with a traditional fire pit. Just some fire wood, a grate to cook on, and lots of delicious food. And what's more rewarding than waking up in a tent, starting a fire, and brewing a big pot of coffee?

Gas Grills—A gas grill is probably the easiest (and perhaps even a cheater method to live fire cooking). The fire is extremely easy to control, and it heats up very quickly. A good gas grill is a terrific way to learn how to cook with live fire.

Hearth Cooking—Hearth cooking is one of the oldest forms of cooking. This method uses a home fireplace with a fire. It's wonderful in the winter, but does require some special equipment and a few adjustments to a traditional fireplace. A fireplace crane with a swivel arm can be attached to the inside of the fireplace to make cooking over the fire easier and safer.

Gaucho Grills—Gaucho grills are used in specialty restaurants a lot, but there are some made for home use and even directions online for building your own. After a fire is built, the grill grate is moved up and down with a crank wheel to control the heat during cooking. These grills are impressive and are based off traditional Argentinean grills.

CLEANING AND MAINTENANCE

To ensure your food is as delicious as it possibly can be, it's best to get in the habit of cleaning and maintaining your equipment often. Each grill or outdoor appliance has different needs, so it's best to read the owner's manual.

GRILLS

For charcoal and kamado grills its good practice to scrape out the remaining charcoal, ash, and wood every three to four uses. Some buildup is good but eventually it needs to be cleaned out.

The grates of any grill should be scrubbed with a wire bristle after each use while the grill is still warm to break off any leftover pieces of food. A quick brush down when the grill heats up before cooking is a good idea too, in order to make sure the grill grate is clean.

If your grill has a grease trap, this should be cleaned or changed out at least every month during grilling season and at the end of the season before winter storage. Nothing is worse than rancid-smelling grease that is attracting bugs to the grill.

WOOD-FIRED PIZZA OVENS

Wood-fired pizza ovens burn extremely hot, so each time the oven is fired it self-cleans. However, sometimes bits of food do get stuck, so using a copper brush on the oven floor will remove any stuck-on food or ash before cooking. Do not use a steel barbecue grill brush (it will scratch the cooking floor) or a natural fiber brush (it will burn).

Cleaning the bottom of the floor isn't necessary before making pizza. Just a good brush to sweep off any ash is all that is needed. However, using a damp towel might be helpful to clean the floor and moderate the temperature, which will reduce scorching. Check the owner's manual for your particular oven to see how to clean the floor of your oven.

If the opening to your pizza oven is getting dark with soot, you can occasionally clean the opening with mild soap, water, and a soft cloth. I personally like the look of the opening slowly darkening over time. Do not use any oven cleaners as they will damage the surface.

Clean out the ash or the old ashes will get in the way of cooking. Let the ash cool completely (this may take a day or two), remove with a metal shovel, and place in a metal container with a tight-fitting lid. Make sure to store the closed container of ash on the ground, well away from all combustible materials. Cold ashes can be buried in soil, locally dispersed to fertilize certain plants and even lawns (don't use any ash that contains charcoal), or placed in a garbage can. There are some great resources online about how to use wood ash as fertilizer. This is best done a day or two after cooking, but can wait until starting a new fire if you prefer.

ACCESSORIES

The following accessories are fun and useful to have. Many of them can be found at big-box and home-improvement stores, online, and anywhere grills are sold.

Grill Baskets—A few good grill baskets will keep smaller items together and food from falling through the slots in the smoker racks.

Long-Handled Basting Brushes or Barbecue Mops—The last thing you want to do is reach into the back of a hot grill to baste your meat. Long-handled brushes or basting mops are a must!

High-Temperature Gloves—Gloves or heavy-duty potholders are another absolute necessity. The smoker gets extremely hot, and removing food and trays can be tricky.

Cast-Iron Cookware—Cast iron heats evenly and is meant to take the abuse that smoking can inflict on pots and pans. I recommend having a couple different sizes, but measure before buying to make sure they will fit inside your grill and/or pizza oven. I suggest having a 10-inch skillet, 8-inch skillet, and a 6- or 8-quart covered Dutch oven on hand.

Standing Chicken Roaster—A vertical roaster is a fun gadget to keep on hand. You can use it in the smoker, on the grill, or in the oven to cook a bird upright. Most versions have a place where you can add a can to make beer-can or soda-can chicken dinners. Cooking chicken vertically helps to keep it moist and allows the skin to crisp up evenly.

Long-Handled Pizza Peels & Pizza Oven Accessories—Several items are a necessity for using a pizza oven. A few must-haves include a rectangular, anodized aluminum rectangular peel, stainless steel round peel, copper brush, and stainless steel rake and shovel. I also keep several regular wooden pizza peels for rolling out the dough and tossing it into the oven, as well as several rolling pins.

Chimney Starter—Using a chimney starter helps alleviate the need for lighter fluid. See page 14 for instructions on using a chimney starter.

Rotisserie Attachment—An electric rotisserie attachment for a kamado, charcoal, or gas grill is a fun addition to outdoor cooking. The result is an extremely moist piece of meat because the meat will baste itself during the cooking process.

Pizza Stone—A pizza stone or two is a must. They are fairly inexpensive and will crisp up pizza crust during the cooking process. They can be used on a gas grill, charcoal grill, kamado grill, and even an indoor oven. The more they are used, the darker (more seasoned) they become. Since pizza stones are porous, it's best not to get them wet. Use a silicon scraper to clean stuck-on pieces of food after the stone has completely cooled.

Small Metal Garbage Pail—A small metal garbage pail with a tight-fitting lid is useful in discarding leftover charcoal, ash, and wood from grills and ovens.

WOOD

It's a good idea to keep a wide selection of wood on hand for live fire cooking, since different types of wood impart different flavors to food. Oak, pecan, cherry, mesquite, and hickory are some of the more widely used varieties. Mesquite and hickory are great all-purpose woods, while pecan is excellent with beef and cherry is perfect with pork. I've specified which wood I like to use for each recipe, but if you don't have those woods on hand or if you want to get creative, feel free to switch it up. It's also fun to combine two types of wood chips for a unique flavor.

WOOD TYPE	USE WITH
ALDER	FISH; GOOD ALL-PURPOSE CHIP
APPLE	CHICKEN, PORK, VEGETABLES, DESSERTS
CHERRY	CHICKEN, PORK, BEEF, DESSERTS
HICKORY	GOOD ALL-PURPOSE CHIP
MAPLE	PORK, BEEF, VEGETABLES, DESSERTS
MESQUITE	GOOD ALL-PURPOSE CHIP
OAK	BEEF, FISH
PECAN	CHICKEN, PORK, BEEF, VEGETABLES

When buying wood for smoking, grilling, or using in a pizza oven it's best to make sure they are safe. Woods to avoid include but are not limited to:

- Pressure-treated wood (it's treated with chemicals)

- Wood composite, plywood, or particle board (it's mixed with glue and sometimes plastic)

- Wood that has any sort of paint, stain, or varnish

- Oleander (it's extremely toxic)
- Camphor
- Castor
- Resinous trees (pine, spruce, evergreens), except oak
- Sumac
- Green wood, or wood that hasn't fully dried
- Unknown wood scraps

CHARCOAL

Charcoal is mostly carbon made by cooking wood in a low-oxygen environment. For cooking, I prefer lump charcoal (mesquite lump charcoal is great to cook over). However, it's best to skip the lighter fluid or charcoal treated with lighter fluid when the plan is to cook over the coals as it tends to impart an unpleasant taste to whatever is being cooked. A chimney starter will help light your charcoal without the use of any lighter fluid.

LIVE FIRE BASICS

The recipes in this book include prep time for the actual recipe and do not include fire building and preheat time because every fire is different depending on the weather, wood, where the fire is build, etc.

HOW TO BUILD A TEEPEE FIRE

To build a simple teepee fire, start by placing some tinder (dry leaves or pine needles) or some wadded-up newspaper in the middle of the fire area. Then place small twigs up against each other until a mini teepee is formed around the tinder. Leave an open space in the center where you can place additional tinder, if needed. Use a long match to light the tinder, which will then travel up to light the twigs. To keep the fire going, continue adding small twigs to the fire. This little fire doesn't produce a lot of heat or cook much, but mastering this starter fire is the first step in creating a larger cooking fire.

A small teepee fire can be used to boil water or make some coffee.

HOW TO BUILD A COOKING FIRE

The beginning of a large cooking fire starts with a basic teepee fire. Once the teepee fire is going nicely, slowly add five to six small logs until the fire is much larger and hot. Once the fire is going well, lay two logs side by side about 7 inches apart at one end, and 4 inches at the other, sort of in a "V" shape. The two logs serve as a stove range where you can place pots and pans, especially if you don't have a cooking grate. You can put your smaller pots or a coffee pot on the narrower end and your larger pots on the wider end. This enables you to cook several dishes at the same time. Spread (or pile) the coals to create hotter or cooler cooking areas depending on your cooking needs. Add more small logs as needed to keep the fire going during the cooking process.

HOW TO OIL A GRILL

Prepare grill as desired for cooking. Pour 2 to 3 tablespoons of vegetable or canola oil in a small bowl. Fold up a paper towel and grab the paper towel with a pair of long grilling thongs. Dip the paper towel in the oil and rub over the grill grate area that will be used for cooking (no need to do the entire grill, unless the whole grill will be used). Go over the area several times, using more oil as needed.

HOW TO USE A CHIMNEY STARTER

To get started, remove the cooking grate from your grill. Loosely wad up a few pieces of newspaper and place them in the bottom of the chimney starter, then fill it three quarters of the way with lump charcoal. Top with wood chunks of choice.

Set the chimney starter on the bottom of the grill, light a match, and place it through the opening on the bottom of the starter so it lights the newspaper. The fire will begin burning the newspaper and then the charcoal will ignite and flames will grow upward toward the wood.

It will take 10 to 15 minutes for the coals to be sufficiently lit and the wood at the top to burn. The coals are ready when the ones near the top have turned a bit gray with ash. Using a fire-resistant glove, grab the handle and dump the charcoal and wood onto the grill. Slowly pour them out based on the type of cooking you will be doing, direct or indirect (two-zone or even three-zone cooking).

For direct cooking, place the coals and wood in the middle of the grill, and for indirect place the coal on two sides, leaving space in the middle or to one side free of coals, depending on what you are cooking. Once the coals are arranged, place the grill grate back in place, close the grill lid, and let the grill heat up for 10 to 15 minutes. Adjust any dampers to fine-tune the cooking temperature. However, indirect cooking isn't true live fire cooking since the cooking is not done with direct heat or fire.

For short cooking times, like for steak or chicken breasts, this should be all the wood and charcoal you need. However, for longer cooking times, plan on adding additional wood and charcoal during the cooking process to maintain your desired temperature.

SAFETY

Live fire requires your full attention as it's easy for a fire to grow large, send off sparks, or harm someone. Use extreme caution and stay aware of your surroundings when cooking with live fire. Always use fireproof gloves and long-handled equipment. Make sure to light the fire in a safe, well-ventilated area that is set up for live fire.

Be sure to read your owner's manual for specific details about the equipment that you are using. When cooking in the forest while camping, obey all fire warnings and only build fires in approved pits.

BREAKFASTS

Apple Pie Monkey Bread

Ooey gooey monkey bread is always a family favorite. Adding apple pie filling makes it amazing! And since you'll be making the monkey bread in the pizza oven, swap biscuits for some pizza dough...trust me, it works! I fire up my pizza oven for pizza almost every Friday night and the oven is still between 400 to 500 degrees the next morning, so it's a great way to bake bread or breakfast or even some desserts.

Prep time: 1 hour | *Cooking time:* 25 minutes | *Serves:* 4 | *Equipment:* pizza oven

1 recipe Classic Pizza Dough
(page 114)

1 cup sugar

2 tablespoons ground cinnamon

6 tablespoons butter, melted

1 (21-ounce) can apple pie filling

1. Prepare a wood-fired pizza oven with a 400°F fire that's been burning for about an hour (or use residual heat in the oven from a previous fire). Spray a metal or cast-iron Bundt pan well with nonstick cooking spray.

2. Allow pizza dough to rest at room temperature for 30 minutes. Meanwhile, in a small bowl, combine sugar and cinnamon coating ingredients. Whisk to blend; set aside.

3. Use a dough cutter to cut pizza dough into 2-inch pieces, then roll each piece gently into a ball shape. Give each dough ball a good roll in the melted butter and then in the cinnamon-sugar mixture. Place in the prepared pan. Make a full circle in the bottom of the pan with the balls.

4. After the bottom is covered in dough balls, evenly spread the apple pie filling all around the pan and first layer of dough balls. Repeat dough ball process and place in an even layer on top of the apple pie filling.

5. Sprinkle any leftover cinnamon-sugar coating over the top of the dough in the baking pan. The monkey bread can go in the refrigerator overnight at this point for a quick and easy breakfast.

6. To bake, place pan in a 400°F pizza oven for 25 minutes to bake. If the oven has an active fire, leave the door open; however, if using residual heat put the oven door back on to trap the heat for cooking.

7. After cooking, allow the monkey bread to sit in the Bundt pan for about 5 minutes before turning it out onto a serving dish or plate. To do this, place the plate upside down on top of the baking pan, and (while wearing oven mitts), quickly turn the plate and baking pan over. The monkey bread should release from the pan without a problem. Let bread cool an additional 10 minutes to allow the syrup to cool before serving.

NOTE: If you are using a prepared Bundt pan from the refrigerator, take out when you preheat the pizza oven and let dough rise for 30 minutes while the oven preheats. Bake as mentioned above.

Sausage & Egg Breakfast Pizza

Breakfast pizza is a new family favorite. Fire up the pizza oven first thing in the morning for some quick breakfasts. I love making these by carefully placing a raw egg in the center of the pizza before putting it into the pizza oven; however, it would be fun to scramble up some eggs and use like a regular pizza topping.

Prep time: *30 minutes* |
Cooking time: *2 minutes* | **Serves:** *4* |
Equipment: *pizza oven*

1 recipe Classic Pizza Dough (page 114)

corn meal and flour, for rolling dough

2 tablespoons extra virgin olive oil

1 pound container bulk breakfast sausage, cooked and drained

1 cup shredded Colby Jack cheese

4 eggs

4 green onions, chopped

salsa, to serve

salt and pepper

1. Prepare a wood-fired pizza oven with a 700 to 800°F fire that's been burning for about an hour.

2. Roll out one of the pizza doughs on a pizza peel that is lightly floured and dusted with corn meal. Brush with olive oil and then top with about one-quarter of the cooked sausage and cheese.

3. Gently crack an egg into the middle of the dough. Lightly season with salt and pepper to taste.

4. Make sure the dough isn't sticking to the pizza peel. Gently place in the pizza oven by sliding it off the pizza peel and cook for 1 minute. Rotate and cook for an additional minute or until crust and egg have reached desired consistency. Top with green onions and salsa.

5. Repeat process with additional pizza dough and ingredients.

Asparagus & Swiss Cheese Quiche

This is great for breakfast or brunch. The creamy Swiss cheese and crunchy asparagus go so well together. Try mixing in grape tomatoes or chopped red peppers for a twist.

Prep time: *15 minutes* | ***Cooking time:*** *20 to 30 minutes* | ***Serves:*** *8* | ***Equipment:*** *pizza oven*

1 refrigerated pie dough

6 eggs

½ cup half and half, whole milk, or heavy cream

1½ cups shredded Swiss cheese

1 teaspoon coarse Kosher salt

1½ to 2 cups chopped asparagus plus 8 whole asparagus spears (about 1 bunch), washed and woody ends trimmed

½ small white onion, finely diced

1. Prepare a wood-fired pizza oven with a 450 to 500°F fire that's been burning for about an hour (or use residual heat in the oven from a previous fire).

2. Spray a 9-inch pie pan with nonstick cooking spray and unroll the pie dough into the pie pan. Set aside.

3. In a large bowl, combine the eggs, half and half, cheese, and salt. Whisk to combine. Add in the chopped asparagus and onion. Stir gently to mix.

4. Pour the egg mixture into the prepared pie pan. Place 8 asparagus spears on top of the egg mixture.

5. Place in pizza oven for 20 to 30 minutes, rotating every 10 minutes, or until top is lightly browned and eggs are set.

NOTE: Quiche could also be made in a kamado grill with a pizza stone and an indirect fire. Time will vary based on the fire temperature.

Cajun Egg Scramble

I make variations of this Cajun egg scramble on every single camping trip. It's easy to prep at home, take camping, and then cook over an open fire. I usually make my own Cajun seasoning blend, but store-bought blends are great too. Try changing up the sausage or cheese for different variations.

Prep time: 20 minutes | Cooking time: 30 minutes | Serves: 4 | Equipment: grill, kamado, or fire pit

8 sausage links

1 tablespoon canola or vegetable oil

½ onion, chopped

½ red bell pepper, chopped

2 cloves garlic, minced

6 eggs

1 teaspoon Cajun Seasoning (page 24)

1 teaspoon chili powder

salt and pepper

1 cup shredded pepper Jack cheese

salsa, flour tortillas, and/or Foiled Blue Cheese Potatoes (page 110)

1. Prepare and light a grill, kamado, or fire pit with a cooking grate for direct cooking over medium heat, and heat a large cast-iron skillet.

2. Place sausage links in the hot skillet and cook, turning often, until fully cooked, about 15 minutes. Once fully cooked, remove from pan to a paper towel–lined plate to absorb some of the excess grease.

3. Add oil, onions, and peppers to the skillet. Cook until soft and starting to caramelize. Add garlic. Cook until fragrant, 30 seconds to 1 minute.

4. In a large bowl, beat eggs and add Cajun seasoning and chili powder. Add to veggie mixture and scramble to desired doneness.

5. Season with salt and pepper to taste, then stir in cheese. Move eggs to one side and add sausage back to the pan to reheat. Serve warm. If desired, serve with salsa and a side of foiled potatoes or wrapped up in a tortilla.

NOTE: To prep to take camping, put each in their own baggies: onions with peppers, minced garlic, sausage, cheese, spices (chili powder, Cajun seasoning, salt, and pepper all in one bag), and oil. Now place all the little baggies into one large baggie and label. Keep the eggs separate in their egg container for safe keeping.

Cajun Seasoning

2 teaspoons coarse Kosher salt

2 teaspoons garlic powder

1½ teaspoons onion powder

1¼ teaspoons dried oregano

1¼ teaspoons dried thyme

½ teaspoon ground black pepper

1 teaspoon cayenne pepper

½ teaspoon red pepper flakes

Mix all ingredients together in a small bowl. Store in a sealed container for up to 3 months.

Cast-Iron Cinnamon Rolls

Delicious, homemade cinnamon rolls in under an hour. There is literally no reason NOT to make these. I love to add ground cloves and allspice to my filling as it gives it just a little extra warmth than cinnamon alone; however, feel free to use extra cinnamon if you aren't a fan. Try adding various chopped nuts or raisins for another option.

Prep time: *30 minutes* | **Cooking time:** *15 to 20 minutes* | **Serves:** *6* | **Equipment:** *grill, kamado, or fire pit*

DOUGH

1 cup warm water

2 tablespoons sugar

2 tablespoons active dry yeast

1 teaspoon coarse Kosher salt

6 tablespoons butter, softened

3 cups unbleached all-purpose flour

FILLING

6 tablespoons butter, softened

6 tablespoons brown sugar, packed

4 teaspoons ground cinnamon

½ teaspoon ground cloves

½ teaspoon ground allspice

FROSTING

4 ounces cream cheese, softened

4 tablespoons butter, melted

3 cups powdered sugar

2 teaspoons vanilla extract

2 to 3 tablespoons milk (whatever type you have on hand)

1. Prepare and light a grill, kamado, or fire pit with a cooking grate for two-zone cooking over medium heat.

2. To make the dough, place the hot water, sugar, and yeast in the bowl of a stand mixer fitted with the paddle attachment. Let the mixture rest for 15 minutes; it will be very frothy.

3. While the yeast blooms, prepare the filling by stirring all the filling ingredients, except the butter, together in a small bowl with a fork. Set aside.

4. Add the salt and butter for the dough to the mixing bowl. Beat on medium using the paddle, until the butter is incorporated into the mixture. Switch to the dough hook and add the flour. Start on low for a few seconds, until the flour starts to incorporate, then switch to medium speed until the dough completely comes together. It's done when all of the dough forms a ball and the sides of the bowl are almost clean (no dough left). If dough is too wet, add an additional tablespoon or two of flour.

5. Roll out dough on a lightly floured surface into a rectangle that's about 11 x 13 inches or so. Spread softened butter over the dough and sprinkle filling mixture evenly over the buttered dough. Roll the dough into a long, tight roll. Cut into 12 equal slices with a serrated knife. Place in a 12-inch cast-iron skillet. Let rest for 5 more minutes.

6. Place cast-iron skillet over direct fire for 10 minutes, rotating after 5 minutes. Then move to indirect heat for another 5 to 10 minutes, or until fully cooked. Watch closely as it will burn quickly.

7. While the cinnamon rolls are on the grill, make the frosting. Whisk the softened cream cheese and melted butter in a medium bowl, then whisk in powdered sugar, vanilla extract, and 2 tablespoons of milk. Add more milk until frosting reaches desired consistency. Frost rolls and serve warm.

APPETIZERS

Bruschetta with Fire-Roasted Tomatoes

Throw some tomatoes on the grill to add a fire-roasted kick to this easy appetizer.

Prep time: *1 hour 45 minutes* | **Cooking time:** *20 minutes* | **Serves:** *10*
| **Equipment:** *grill, kamado, or fire pit*

8 Roma tomatoes

¼ teaspoon coarse Kosher salt

2 cloves garlic

1 French baguette, thinly sliced

12 large fresh basil leaves, thinly sliced

½ tablespoon extra virgin olive oil

1. Prepare and light a grill, kamado, or fire pit with a cooking grate for direct cooking over medium-high heat.

2. Blister tomatoes over a hot fire for about 5 minutes on each side. This usually takes about 20 minutes total. Remove tomatoes from fire, place in a bowl, and chill in the refrigerator for an hour.

3. Remove chilled tomatoes from refrigerator, slice in half, and remove seeds. Chop tomatoes into pieces, then place in a colander with ¼ teaspoon of salt over a bowl. The juice will drain out of the tomatoes so that the mixture isn't too wet when placed on the baguette slices.

4. While the tomatoes drain, slice garlic cloves in half and rub cut halves onto one side of each piece of sliced baguette.

5. In a medium bowl combine drained tomatoes, sliced basil, and olive oil. Gently stir to combine, taste, and adjust salt, if needed.

6. Place a small spoonful of tomato basil mixture on each piece of bread. Serve immediately.

Grilled Blue Cheese Wedge Salad

Wedge salads are always a fun way to eat a salad. There are so many delicious toppings on a classic wedge salad, but throwing the lettuce on the grill to get a little bit of char on the leaves really takes this salad to another level.

Prep time: *30 minutes* | **Cooking time:** *25 minutes* | **Serves:** *4* | **Equipment:** *grill, kamado, or fire pit*

2 heads romaine lettuce, halved longwise

2 tablespoons extra virgin olive oil

6 slices cooked bacon, crumbled

2 tomatoes, diced

2 tablespoons chopped fresh chives

4 tablespoons blue cheese crumbles

blue cheese or ranch dressing, to taste

Balsamic Glaze (see below)

1. Prepare and light a grill, kamado, or fire pit with a cooking grate for direct cooking over medium heat.

2. Brush the romaine heads on the cut edges with a little olive oil. Place over direct medium heat for 5 minutes per side, 10 minutes total.

3. Place each wedge of lettuce on a plate and top with the bacon crumbles, diced tomatoes, chopped chives, and blue cheese crumbles. Add your favorite blue cheese or ranch and then drizzle with 1 to 2 teaspoons of balsamic glaze.

Balsamic Glaze

⅓ cup balsamic vinegar

2 tablespoons sugar

Place ingredients in a small pot and bring to a boil over medium-high heat for 5 minutes, then reduce to a simmer for 10 minutes or until glaze has reduced by half. Stir occasionally. Serve warm or at room temperature.

Tomatillo Salsa

This is one of my family's favorite salsas. It's a little sweet and a little spicy. It's great for dipping or adding to enchiladas or tacos for some extra flavor. Don't let the tomatillos scare you away from making this amazing salsa.

Prep time: 15 minutes, plus several hours to overnight to marinate | Cooking time: 30 minutes | Serves: 6 | Equipment: grill, kamado, or fire pit

2 pounds (about 15 large) green tomatillos, husks removed

2 jalapeños

6 to 8 cloves garlic

1 sweet onion

½ bunch fresh cilantro, leaves only

¼ cup sugar

½ cup vegetable stock

coarse Kosher salt

tortilla chips, for serving

1. Prepare and light a grill, kamado, or fire pit with a cooking grate for direct cooking over medium heat.

2. Grill tomatillos and jalapeños until darkened and blistered, about 30 minutes. Put the jalapeños into a plastic bag for 5 minutes and then peel off darkened skin. Let everything cool to room temperature.

3. Place garlic and onion in food processor. Process until finely chopped. Add remaining ingredients and process until the desired consistency is reached. Season to taste with salt and/or sugar if desired.

4. Store in the refrigerator for several hours or overnight to let the flavors develop.

5. Serve cold with tortilla chips.

Black Bean Campfire Nachos

Nachos are pure comfort food! There are so many great ways to make them, and they are perfect for leftovers too. Have leftover ground beef or carne asada? Feel free to add it in. These nachos are ready in 15 minutes and make a great lunch, dinner, or even an afternoon snack.

Prep time: 5 minutes | Cooking time: 10 minutes | Serves: 4 | Equipment: fire pit

1 (10-ounce) bag tortilla chips, divided

1 (14-ounce) can black beans, drained and rinsed, divided

1 (14.5-ounce) can diced tomatoes, drained, divided

1 cup salsa, divided

2 cups shredded cheddar cheese, divided

2 cups shredded Colby Jack cheese, divided

3 green onions, sliced

1 avocado, sliced

½ cup sliced black olives

½ cup roughly chopped cup fresh cilantro

1 jalapeño, sliced

juice of ½ lime

seasoned ground beef, sour cream, diced red bell peppers, optional

1. Prepare a fire in a fire pit that has a cooking grate.

2. In a 12-inch cast-iron skillet, evenly layer half of the chips, followed by half of the beans, tomatoes, and salsa. Top with 1 cup cheddar and 1 cup Colby Jack cheese.

3. Repeat all layers again until remaining ingredients have been used, except for the green onions, avocado, black olives, cilantro, jalapeño, and lime.

4. Cover the skillet with aluminum foil and let cook for 10 minutes or until the cheese melts. Remove from heat, uncover, top with avocado, black olives, cilantro, jalapeño, and a squeeze of lime. Add seasoned ground beef, sour cream, or red bell peppers, if desired.

Bacon-Wrapped Dates

These bite-sized appetizers are usually the first thing to be eaten at any party; they are great cooked over mesquite wood or mesquite lump charcoal.

Prep time: *30 minutes* | **Cooking time:** *20 minutes* | **Serves:** *12* | **Equipment:** *grill, kamado, or fire pit*

36 dates, pitted

36 roasted almonds

12 slices bacon, cut into thirds

36 toothpicks, if desired

maple syrup, slightly warmed for brushing

1. Prepare and light a grill, kamado, or fire pit with a cooking grate for direct cooking over medium heat.

2. Gently slice into a date, separating the halves (but keeping opposite side intact, butterflying the date). Place an almond inside the date and squish date halves back together. Repeat with all remaining dates.

3. Take a small piece of bacon and wrap it around each date, securing with a toothpick if needed. Place in a wire basket.

4. Brush each date with warm maple syrup and grill over direct medium heat for 7 minutes. Turn dates over and grill for an additional 7 minutes, then turn dates one last time and grill for 5 to 6 more minutes or until bacon is browned and crispy. Baste dates with maple syrup every 5 minutes.

5. Remove from wire basket and enjoy warm (or at room temperature).

MAIN DISHES

Flank Steak with Chimichurri Sauce

Cooking a big flank steak is great for a party or big family supper. Adding a homemade chimichurri sauce really elevates the flavor of this steak.

Prep time: 10 minutes, plus 1 hour to marinate | Cooking time: 10 minutes | Serves: 4 | Equipment: grill, kamado, or fire pit

2 tablespoons extra virgin olive oil

1½- to 2-pound flank steak

2 cloves garlic, finely minced

½ tablespoon coarse Kosher salt

¼ tablespoon ground black pepper

juice of 1 small lemon

Chimichurri Sauce (see below), to serve

1. Place all ingredients in a zip-top gallon bag. Seal, and place in the refrigerator for at least 1 hour. Flip bag every 15 to 20 minutes.

2. Prepare and light a grill, kamado, or fire pit with a cooking grate for direct cooking over high heat.

3. Remove steak from bag and grill over direct heat for 10 minutes for medium to medium-well doneness, flipping halfway through the cooking time. Continue cooking until desired doneness is achieved.

Chimichurri Sauce

2 tablespoons red wine vinegar

1 teaspoon coarse Kosher salt

4 cloves garlic

¼ cup fresh cilantro

1 cup fresh parsley

2 tablespoons fresh oregano

⅓ cup extra virgin olive oil

½ teaspoon red pepper flakes

Place all the ingredients in a food processor or heavy-duty blender and pulse until combined and herbs are broken down, but still have a little texture. Serve immediately.

Carne Asada

This Tex-Mex beef is easy, but needs up to 24 hours to marinate. The longer it marinates, the better. This is also a great recipe for camping since it can be made a day or two in advance and then thrown on the grill.

Prep time: 30 minutes, plus 12 to 24 hours to marinate | Cooking time: 14 to 20 minutes | Serves: 6 to 8 | Equipment: grill, kamado, or fire pit

¾ cup orange juice

½ cup lemon juice

½ cup soy sauce

½ cup extra virgin olive oil

⅓ cup fresh lime juice

6 cloves garlic, minced

2 tablespoons white vinegar

1 tablespoon chili powder

1 tablespoon ground cumin

1 teaspoon paprika

1 teaspoon dried oregano

1 teaspoon ground black pepper

1 bunch fresh cilantro, chopped

1 jalapeño, minced

3 pounds boneless round or chuck roast, thinly sliced

corn tortillas, pico de gallo, sour cream, avocado, and cheese, to serve

1. Combine all the ingredients, including the thinly sliced roast, in a zip-top gallon bag. Seal and squeeze it around to mix it up, then place in the refrigerator for 12 to 24 hours.

2. Prepare and light a grill, kamado, or fire pit with a cooking grate for direct cooking over medium heat.

3. Remove the roast slices from the marinade, and discard excess marinade. Cook on the grill for 7 to 10 minutes per side.

4. Once done, remove from heat and let rest 10 minutes. Slice against the grain and serve with corn tortillas and toppings as desired.

Beefy Lasagna

Take your traditional lasagna up a notch with some smoky goodness. We used pecan wood in our pizza oven and kamado to give a nice smoky flavor. Once you make this smoked Beefy Lasagna you may never turn on your oven for lasagna again.

Prep time: 30 minutes | *Cooking time:* 1 hour 30 minutes | *Serves:* 8 to 10 | *Equipment:* pizza oven

1 pound mild Italian sausage

2 pounds ground beef

1 (29-ounce) can tomato sauce

1 (12-ounce) can tomato paste

1½ cups water

1 medium onion, finely diced

6 cloves garlic, minced

1¼ teaspoons ground black pepper, divided

⅓ cup brown sugar, packed

3 tablespoons Worcestershire sauce

3 tablespoons chili powder

3 tablespoons lemon juice

3 teaspoons dried oregano

1½ tablespoons plus 1 teaspoon coarse Kosher salt, divided

9 lasagna noodles

1 teaspoon dried parsley

1 teaspoon garlic powder

1 large egg, lightly beaten

1 (15-ounce) carton ricotta cheese

4 to 6 cups shredded part-skim mozzarella cheese, divided

¾ cup grated Parmesan cheese, divided

1. Prepare a wood-fired pizza oven with pecan wood and a 500°F fire that's been burning for about an hour.

2. In a large stockpot, brown the Italian sausage and ground beef until cooked through. Drain off fat and add tomato sauce, tomato paste, water, onion, garlic, ¾ teaspoon black pepper, brown sugar, Worcestershire sauce, chili powder, lemon juice, oregano, and 1½ tablespoons salt. Stir well to combine. Bring to a simmer over medium heat.

3. Stir, cover, and reduce heat to low to simmer for at least an hour. Stir occasionally. Taste and adjust seasonings as needed.

4. Meanwhile, cook noodles according to package directions; drain.

5. In a small bowl, mix parsley, garlic powder, remaining 1 teaspoon salt and ½ teaspoon black pepper, egg, and ricotta cheese.

6. Spread 2 cups meat sauce into a 13 x 9-inch baking dish that has been sprayed with nonstick cooking spray. Layer with three noodles and a third of the ricotta mixture. Sprinkle with 1 cup mozzarella cheese and 2 tablespoons Parmesan cheese. Repeat layers twice. Top with remaining meat sauce and cheeses (dish will be very full).

7. Place in pizza oven for 20 minutes, rotating halfway through the cooking time. Check for doneness after around 15 minutes. If an active fire is burning, keep pizza oven door open; however, if using residual heat close the door to trap the heat. (This can also be made in a 375°F to 400°F kamado grill using lump charcoal and pecan wood with an indirect fire for 40 to 60 minutes. Keep the lid closed to trap the heat, but check on lasagna every 5 to 10 minutes after the 30-minute mark).

8. Let lasagna cool for 10 to 15 minutes before serving.

NOTE: There will be extra meat sauce after the lasagna is assembled. This makes a great topping for spaghetti, or use for another smaller lasagna. It also freezes well for up to 2 months.

Stuffed Green Chili & Cheese Burgers

Nothing beats fresh roasted chilies, but canned ones also work great in this stuffed burger.

Prep time: *30 minutes* | ***Cooking time:*** *10 minutes* | ***Serves:*** *4*
| ***Equipment:*** *grill, kamado, or fire pit*

1½ pounds 85% lean ground beef

½ teaspoon coarse Kosher salt

¼ teaspoon garlic powder

⅛ teaspoon ground black pepper

1 (4-ounce) can diced green chilies or ½ cup

diced roasted fresh green chilies, divided

1 cup shredded sharp cheddar cheese, divided

4 brioche buns

lettuce, tomato, and onion, to serve, optional

1. In a large bowl, combine ground beef, salt, garlic powder, and black pepper. Mix with hands or wooden spoon to combine. Form beef into 8 balls.

2. Using hands, press 1 ball flat and place 1 tablespoon of green chilies and ¼ cup of cheese in the middle. Take a second ball, flatten it, and place on top of the bacon and cheese mixture. Press the sides of both patties together, pinching the seams together tightly so the filling doesn't ooze out while cooking.

3. Prepare and light a grill, kamado, or fire pit with a cooking grate for direct cooking over medium-high heat.

4. Cook burgers for 5 minutes per side for medium to medium-well doneness. Place burgers on buns and top as desired with lettuce, onion, and tomato.

NOTE: Do not press burgers with a spatula while cooking or all the filling will come out of the sides.

Stuffed Blue Cheese Bacon Burgers

These are the first stuffed burgers I ever made and they are still my favorite to this day! The blue cheese becomes warm and gooey in the center of the burger.

Prep time: 30 minutes | Cooking time: 10 minutes | Serves: 4 | Equipment: grill, kamado, or fire pit

1½ pounds 85% lean ground beef

½ teaspoon coarse Kosher salt

¼ teaspoon garlic powder

⅛ teaspoon ground black pepper

6 slices cooked bacon, crumbled, divided

1 cup crumbled blue cheese, divided

4 brioche buns

lettuce, onion, and tomato, to serve, optional

1. In a large bowl, combine ground beef, salt, garlic powder, and black pepper. Mix with hands or a wooden spoon to combine. Form beef into 8 balls.

2. Using hands, press 1 ball flat and place one-quarter of the bacon and ¼ cup cheese in the middle. Take a second ball, flatten it, and place on top of the bacon and cheese mixture. Press the sides of both patties together, pinching the seams together tightly so the filling doesn't ooze out while cooking. Repeat process with remaining patties.

3. Prepare and light a grill, kamado, or fire pit with a cooking grate for direct cooking over medium-high heat.

4. Cook burgers for 5 minutes per side for medium to medium-well doneness. Place burgers on buns and top as desired with lettuce, onion, and tomato.

NOTE: Do not press burgers with a spatula while cooking or all the filling will come out of the sides.

Jalapeño Popper Burgers

If you love jalapeño poppers then this burger is for you! It's full of jalapeño flavor and the cream cheese keeps the heat level in check. Topping with fried jalapeños really takes this burger from great to amazing.

Prep time: *30 minutes* | **Cooking time:** *10 minutes* | **Serves:** *4* | **Equipment:** *grill, kamado, or fire pit*

1½ pounds 85% lean ground beef

2 tablespoons steak seasoning

4 ounces cream cheese, softened

¼ teaspoon coarse Kosher salt

⅛ teaspoon garlic powder

1 (4-ounce) can (about ¼ cup) diced jalapeños

4 hamburger buns

½ cup fried jalapeños

lettuce, onion, and tomato, to serve, optional

1. In a large bowl, combine ground beef and steak seasoning. Mix with hands or wooden spoon to combine. Form beef into 4 balls. Using hands, press 1 ball flat into a round patty. Repeat process with remaining balls.

2. Prepare and light a grill, kamado, or fire pit with a cooking grate for direct cooking over medium-high heat.

3. In a small bowl, combine softened cream cheese, salt, garlic powder, and jalapeños. Stir well to combine. Set aside.

4. Cook burgers for 5 minutes per side for medium to medium-well doneness. Spread cream cheese mixture on one-half of each bun. Place burgers on buns and top with some fried jalapeños, then top as desired with lettuce, onion, and tomato.

NOTE: Do not press burgers with a spatula while cooking or all the juices will escape. You can make your own fried jalapeños, but they are also available near the fried onions and greens beans in the grocery store.

BBQ Bacon & Onion Cheeseburgers

My favorite thing to get when we go out for burgers is a BBQ Bacon Cheeseburger. It's topped with bacon, cheese, and onion rings and is so messy, but totally delicious. This is my version at home using store-bought friend onions.

Prep time: *30 minutes* | ***Cooking time:*** *10 minutes* | ***Serves:*** *4*
| ***Equipment:*** *grill, kamado, or fire pit*

1½ pounds 85% lean ground beef

2 tablespoons steak seasoning

4 slices cheddar cheese

½ cup barbecue sauce, plus more for serving

4 hamburger buns

8 slices cooked bacon

½ cup fried onions

lettuce, onion, and tomato, to serve, optional

1. In a large bowl, combine ground beef and steak seasoning. Mix with hands or wooden spoon to combine. Form beef into 4 balls. Using hands, press 1 ball flat into a round patty. Repeat process with remaining balls.

2. Prepare and light a grill, kamado, or fire pit with a cooking grate for direct cooking over medium-high heat.

3. Cook burgers for 5 minutes per side for medium to medium-well doneness, basting burgers as they cook with barbecue sauce.

4. When burgers are almost done, add a slice of cheese to each burger and let the cheese melt before removing from the grill.

5. Place burgers on buns with 2 slices of bacon, some fried onions, a drizzle of barbecue sauce, and then top as desired with lettuce, onion, and tomato.

NOTE: Do not press burgers with a spatula while cooking or all the juices will escape. You can make your own fried or caramelized onions, but fried onions are also found in the grocery store, usually near the canned green beans.

Honey Garlic Pork Chops

Pork chops are a great weeknight meal because they are a lean protein and cook fast. These chops are on the table in under 30 minutes. Add some grilled vegetables like broccoli or asparagus for a healthy dinner.

Prep time: *5 minutes* | **Cooking time:** *14 to 18 minutes* | **Serves:** *4* | **Equipment:** *grill, kamado, or fire pit*

½ cup ketchup

3 tablespoons honey

2 tablespoons low-sodium soy sauce

2 tablespoons (about 6 cloves) minced garlic

4 bone-in pork loin chops (about 3 to 4 pounds)

1 tablespoon coarse Kosher salt

2 teaspoons ground black pepper

1. Prepare and light a grill, kamado, or fire pit with a cooking grate for direct cooking over medium heat.

2. In a small bowl, whisk the ketchup, honey, soy sauce, and garlic together in a bowl.

3. Season pork chops on both sides with salt and pepper. Sear pork chops on both sides on the preheated grill. Lightly brush glaze onto each side of the chops as they cook, grilling until they are no longer pink in the center, 7 to 9 minutes per side. An instant-read thermometer inserted into the center should read 145°F for medium-rare or 150°F for medium.

4. Rest for 3 minutes under a tinfoil tent before serving.

Brown Sugar & Bourbon Baby Back Ribs

Grab some napkins because these ribs are sticky! They're sweet with a hint of bourbon and cinnamon. Make more than you think you'll need because they'll go fast.

Prep time: 30 minutes | Cooking time: 1½ to 2 hours | Serves: 4 | Equipment: grill, kamado, or fire pit

1 tablespoon coarse Kosher salt

1 tablespoon brown sugar, packed

1½ teaspoons dry mustard

1½ teaspoons dried thyme

½ teaspoon ground ginger

½ teaspoon ground cinnamon

½ teaspoon cayenne pepper

2 (2- to 2¼-pound) racks baby back pork ribs

GLAZE

1 cup dark brown sugar, packed

1 cup cola

1 tablespoon dry mustard

1 tablespoon apple cider vinegar

¼ teaspoon ground black pepper

¼ cup bourbon whiskey

1. Prepare and light a grill, kamado, or fire pit with a cooking grate for direct cooking over medium heat. For longer cooking, adding several pieces of lump charcoal to help the fire stay hot.

2. In a small bowl combine the first 7 ingredients, and stir to combine. Remove ribs from packaging and remove the skin on the back of the ribs, if desired. Pat ribs dry and liberally apply prepared rub.

3. Place ribs on prepared grill over direct heat. Flip and rotate ribs every 20 minutes or so while cooking for 1½ to 2 hours or until ribs are tender and fully cooked.

4. Meanwhile, prepare the glaze. In a medium saucepan, combine the brown sugar, cola, dry mustard, vinegar, and pepper. Bring to boiling, stirring to dissolve brown sugar. Reduce heat. Simmer, uncovered, about 20 minutes or until reduced to about ¾ cup. Remove from heat; stir in whiskey.

5. Brush ribs with some of the glaze during the last 30 minutes of grilling. Ribs are done when they are tender and the bones are sticking out of the ends by about half an inch, 1½ to 2 hours. Serve with the remaining glaze.

Southwestern Rotisserie Pork Loin

Nothing will ever be as juicy as a piece of meat cooked with a rotisserie. As it turns, it self-bastes, keeping it moist and juicy. It's amazing, just like this Southwestern rub that's a little sweet, a little spicy, and perfect for a Sunday dinner. The Southwestern rub recipe makes a lot, so save the leftovers for next time. It would be fabulous on chicken or even some ribs.

Prep time: 5 minutes | *Cooking time:* 1 to 1 hour 30 minutes | *Serves:* 4 to 6
| *Equipment:* rotisserie grill

4½ teaspoons coarse Kosher salt

4 tablespoons brown sugar, packed

1 tablespoon smoked paprika

1 tablespoon ground black pepper

4 teaspoons ground cumin

2 teaspoons garlic powder

2 teaspoons onion powder

2 tablespoons chili powder

2 teaspoons dried oregano

2 teaspoons ground coriander

1 teaspoon cayenne pepper

1 (3- to 3½-pound) pork loin

1. In a small bowl, combine the first 11 ingredients to make a rub.

2. Remove pork loin from packaging and pat dry. Add the rub liberally all over the entire pork loin. (Only about half the rub will be used depending on the size of pork loin. Store remainder in an airtight container.)

3. Prep the grill for the rotisserie, removing grates if you need to and placing a piece of tinfoil or a small tinfoil pan in the middle to catch the drippings. Prepare a medium-high indirect fire with fire on both sides of where the pork loin will be. Plan to replenish the wood every 20 minutes or so during the cooking time to keep the fire hot (or use all lump charcoal for a longer-lasting heat source).

4. Follow grill instructions to place loin securely on the spit, using butcher's twine if necessary. Turn on the rotisserie and grill over indirect heat with the lid closed for 60 to 90 minutes or until internal temperature is 155 to 160°F degrees.

5. Slide the pork loin off the spit and onto a platter. Let the meat rest under a tinfoil tent for 8 to 10 minutes before slicing.

NOTE: A good rule of thumb is to plan on cooking for 20 minutes per pound of pork loin.

Strawberry–Glazed Pork Tenderloin

I love serving fruit with pork, but basting it with a combination of brown mustard and strawberry jam is truly scrumptious. This tenderloin is definitely a crowd pleaser. Serve with a green salad and grilled vegetables for a delicious meal.

Prep time: 15 minutes | Cooking time: 20 to 25 minutes | Serves: 6 to 8 | Equipment: grill, kamado, or fire pit

1 (10- to 12-ounce) jar (about 1½ cups) strawberry jam

¼ cup spicy brown mustard

1 teaspoon coarse Kosher salt, divided

2 (12-ounce) pork tenderloins, trimmed of silver skin and excess fat

1 tablespoon extra virgin olive oil

½ teaspoon ground black pepper

1. Prepare and light a grill, kamado, or fire pit with a cooking grate for direct cooking over medium heat.

2. In a small saucepan, whisk together the jam, mustard, and ¼ teaspoon salt over medium heat until jam melts, 3 to 4 minutes.

3. Remove from heat and transfer half to a small bowl for basting. Cover pan with remaining sauce to keep warm.

4. Rub pork with oil and season with remaining salt and pepper. Place the tenderloins on the grill over direct heat and cook until the pork reaches 150°F on an instant-read thermometer. Turn tenderloins every 5 minutes to brown all sides 15 to 20 minutes total, until the pork reaches 150°F on an instant-read thermometer. During the last minutes of cooking, brush the pork with the reserved sauce on all sides.

5. Cover tenderloin loosely with foil; let rest 5 minutes before slicing. Serve drizzled with remaining warm sauce.

NOTE: This is a great recipe to use up the last of the strawberry jam in a large container.

Beer Brats & Onions

This will become your new favorite way to cook brats! Use your favorite beer or any dark beer to add a layer of flavor to grilled brats.

Prep time: 10 minutes | Cooking time: 15 minutes | Serves: 6 to 8 | Equipment: grill, kamado, or fire pit

1 package (6 to 8) bratwurst sausages

5 cloves garlic, smashed

1 large onion, thinly sliced

2 (12-ounce) cans dark beer (I used Negra Modelo)

6 to 8 hot dog buns or French rolls

mustard, to serve

sauerkraut, to serve, optional

1. Prepare and light a grill, kamado, or fire pit with a cooking grate for direct cooking over medium-high heat.

2. Meanwhile, poke each bratwurst with a fork 2 or 3 times. In a large saucepan, combine bratwurst, garlic, onion, and beer over medium-high heat. Let the bratwurst boil for 5 minutes.

3. Remove bratwurst from beer (let the beer/onion mixture continue boiling) and place on the grill to finish cooking, about 10 minutes, turning often to prevent burning. Remove onions from beer with a slotted spoon and transfer to a serving bowl.

4. Serve bratwurst hot in a bun. Top with mustard and onions and/or sauerkraut, if desired.

Gyro Lamb Meatballs

These meatballs taste just like gyro meat, without all the work and fuss.

Prep time: 10 minutes, plus 1 hour to rest | *Cooking time:* 16 minutes | *Serves:* 4 |
Equipment: grill, kamado, or fire pit

1 pound ground lamb

½ small yellow onion, finely minced

2 cloves garlic, finely minced

2 teaspoons coarse Kosher salt

1 teaspoon dried oregano

½ teaspoon ground black pepper

1. In a medium bowl, combine all the ingredients, mixing together with hands gently until just combined. Place bowl in the refrigerator for 1 hour to let the flavors combine and to allow the meat to rest.

2. Prepare and light a grill, kamado, or fire pit with a cooking grate for direct cooking over medium heat. Spray a grill basket with nonstick cooking spray and set aside.

3. Use a cookie scoop to scoop lamb mixture into hand and gently roll into 12 balls. Work meat as little as possible. Place meatballs into prepared grill basket.

4. Grill over a medium fire with direct heat for 4 minutes per side, about 16 minutes total. Meatballs should be lightly browned. Remove from heat and serve immediately with gyro toppings such as tomato, red onion, feta cheese, and tzatziki sauce.

Lamb Chops with Mint Pesto

Move over mint jelly! The mint pesto with these lamb chops will be your new favorite. Plan on at least two lamb rib chops and a decent-size portion of mint pesto per person. The lamb rib chops are small, so they cook up fast, which makes them a perfect weeknight meal option.

Prep time: 15 minutes | *Cooking time:* 8 to 10 minutes | *Serves:* 4 | *Equipment:* grill, kamado, or fire pit

MINT PESTO

¼ cup slivered almonds

¾ cup mint leaves

3 cloves garlic

¼ cup fresh-squeezed lemon juice plus zest of 1 lemon

⅓ cup extra virgin olive oil

2 tablespoons grated Parmesan cheese

⅛ cup fresh parsley

½ teaspoon coarse Kosher salt

RUB

½ teaspoon coarse Kosher salt

¼ teaspoon ground black pepper

¼ teaspoon garlic powder

¼ teaspoon onion powder

8 lamb rib chops, about 2 pounds total

1. Prepare and light a grill, kamado, or fire pit with a cooking grate for direct cooking over medium-high heat.

2. While the grill heats up, prepare the Mint Pesto by combining everything in a blender or food processor and processing in short bursts until everything is combined and an even consistency. Set aside pesto.

3. Combine salt, pepper, garlic powder, and onion powder in a small bowl. Sprinkle on both sides of each lamb chop to season. Place lamb chops directly on the hot grill over direct heat.

4. Cook lamb for 8 to 10 minutes, flipping and halfway through the cooking time (the internal temperature when done should be 145°F for medium-rare 160°F medium).

5. Serve hot with fresh Mint Pesto.

Greek Lamb Kabobs

Oregano and lemon are my favorite Greek flavors, and they are perfect with the earthy, sweet lamb in these easy kabobs. Serve over a green salad, rice, or my favorite—warm pita bread.

Prep time: 30 minutes, plus 4 to 6 hours to marinate | Cooking time: 12 to 15 minutes | Serves: 6 to 8 | Equipment: grill, kamado, or fire pit

1 (2-pound) boneless lamb leg or shoulder, cut into 1- to 2-inch chunks

5 to 6 tablespoons extra virgin olive oil

6 cloves garlic, crushed

juice of 1 large lemon

1 teaspoon dried oregano

1 teaspoon dried thyme

1 teaspoon coarse Kosher salt

½ teaspoon ground black pepper

6 to 8 wooden skewers

Tzatziki Sauce (see below)

1. Combine lamb, olive oil, garlic, lemon juice, oregano, thyme, salt, and pepper in a zip-top gallon bag. Seal, and squish to coat all the meat. Place in the refrigerator for 4 to 6 hours. Meanwhile soak wooden skewers in water for at least 1 hour.

2. Drain meat and thread lamb onto skewers.

3. Prepare and light a grill, kamado, or fire pit with a cooking grate for direct cooking over medium heat.

4. Grill on medium heat for 12 to 15 minutes or to the desired degree of doneness. Turn kabobs several times to cook evenly.

5. Serve with warm pita bread and Tzatziki Sauce.

Tzatziki Sauce

6 ounces plain yogurt

2 teaspoons lemon juice

½ medium cucumber, peeled, shredded, and juice drained

1 teaspoon finely chopped fresh mint leaves

4 cloves garlic, minced

coarse Kosher salt and ground black pepper, to taste

Put all of the ingredients in a mixing bowl and combine with a fork. Refrigerate for at least 1 hour to allow flavors to marry.

Garlic Herb Rack of Lamb

A rack of lamb is such an impressive-looking dish. This recipe can easily be scaled up for a larger crowd or kept small for a lovely family supper. Adding a few leaves of mint to the rub really adds a ton of flavor.

Prep time: *30 minutes* | **Cooking time:** *20 to 26 minutes* | **Serves:** *4* | **Equipment:** *grill, kamado, or fire pit*

4 cloves garlic, finely minced

2 tablespoons finely chopped fresh thyme

1 tablespoon finely chopped fresh rosemary (or 1 teaspoon dried)

1 teaspoon finely chopped mint leaves

½ teaspoon coarse Kosher salt

¼ teaspoon ground black pepper

1 teaspoon light brown sugar, packed

1½ tablespoons extra virgin olive oil

1 (8-rib) frenched rack of lamb (each rack 1½ pounds), trimmed of all but a thin layer of fat

1. Prepare and light a grill, kamado, or fire pit with a cooking grate for two-zone cooking (one area with a medium heat fire and another for indirect cooking).

2. In a small bowl, combine the garlic, thyme, rosemary, mint, salt, pepper, and brown sugar. Stir in the olive oil. Rub liberally all over the rack of lamb.

3. Place the lamb fat-side down on the hot side of the grill for 3 minutes, and then flip and cook for 3 more minutes to seal in the juices and flavor.

4. Transfer to indirect heat side of the grill and cook with lid down, for an additional 12 to 20 minutes, flipping once or twice for even cooking. Cook until the internal temperature is 140°F (rare), 145°F (medium-rare) or until desired doneness is reached.

5. Remove from grill, place under a tinfoil tent, and allow to rest 10 minutes before slicing to serve.

NOTE: To keep the bones from burning, cover with a piece of tinfoil either before cooking or during the cooking process if they are beginning to char.

Rotisserie Boneless Leg of Lamb

The fresh herbs and lemon juice pair well with the mild gamey flavor of lamb. Cooking it over a fire with a rotisserie keeps it moist and doesn't require a lot of hands-on work.

Prep time: 15 minutes | *Cooking time:* 40 to 60 minutes | *Serves:* 4 | *Equipment:* rotisserie grill

½ cup loosely packed fresh flat-leaf parsley leaves

¼ cup loosely packed fresh rosemary leaves

⅛ cup loosely packed fresh thyme leaves

1 large shallot, quartered

8 cloves garlic

3½ teaspoons coarse Kosher salt

1 tablespoon fresh lemon juice

2 teaspoons ground black pepper

¼ cup extra virgin olive oil

1 (4- to 5-pound) boneless leg of lamb, rolled and tied

1. Prep the grill for the rotisserie, removing grates if you need to and placing a piece of tinfoil or a small tinfoil pan in the middle to catch the drippings.

2. Prepare a medium-high indirect fire with fire on both sides of where the lamb will be. Plan to replenish the wood every 20 minutes or so during the cooking time to keep the fire hot (or use all lump charcoal for a longer-lasting heat source).

3. Place first 8 ingredients in a food processor or blender and pulse until finely chopped. Add olive oil and pulse until smooth, scraping down sides as needed. Rub mixture over lamb.

4. Run spit of the rotisserie through middle of lamb and secure ends with rotisserie forks.

5. Cover and grill for 40 to 60 minutes or until a meat thermometer inserted into thickest portion (avoiding the spit) registers 145°F for medium-rare, 160°F for medium, or 170°F for well-done (stop cooking about 10 degrees before desired doneness as the lamb will continue cooking while resting).

6. Remove lamb from rotisserie, cover loosely with aluminum foil, and let rest 15 minutes before removing the spit and slicing.

Jerk Chicken in Individual Packets

I created a smoked fish version of this jerk chicken in my first cookbook, *Smoke It Like a Pit Master with Your Electric Smoker*. It is such a family favorite, I now regularly make it with chicken in packets for camping. Just a little pre-camping prep work makes this an easy recipe for a campfire. It also works well on a regular grill.

Prep time: 20 minutes, plus 30 minutes to 1 hour to marinate | Cooking time: 15 minutes | Serves: 4 | Equipment: grill, kamado, or fire pit

5 cloves garlic

1 small onion

3 jalapeños, seeded (or leave seeds to make it spicier)

3 teaspoons ground ginger

3 tablespoons light brown sugar, packed

3 teaspoons dried thyme

2 teaspoons coarse Kosher salt

2 teaspoons ground cinnamon

1 teaspoon ground black pepper

1 teaspoon ground allspice

¼ teaspoon cayenne powder

¼ cup extra virgin olive oil

4 (4- to 6-ounce) boneless skinless chicken breasts, sliced into 2 strips each

2 cups sliced carrots

1 bunch green onions, whole

1. In a blender or food processor bowl, combine the first 12 ingredients (garlic through oil), and purée well.

2. Place the chicken pieces in a large zip-top bag, then add the puréed mixture. Seal and gently press the bag to coat the chicken pieces with the marinade. Let marinate for 30 minutes to 1 hour in the refrigerator.

3. Prepare 4 approximately 9 x 13-inch pieces of foil. Divide the ¼ cup of carrots and green onions across the bottom of each piece of foil, and arrange 2 pieces of chicken on top of each. Bring the edges of foil together and gently fold down to seal (leaving a little pocket of air).

4. Prepare and light a grill, kamado, or fire pit with a cooking grate for indirect (two-zone) cooking with medium heat.

5. Cook chicken packets over direct heat for 15 minutes, flipping and rotating several times during the cooking process to cook the chicken evenly. Chicken is done when the juices run clear and has an internal temperature of 165°F.

Lemon Garlic Chicken Legs

These are simple enough for busy weeknights. Just mix everything in a large bag in the morning to marinate then throw on the grill for a quick supper that everyone will love.

Prep time: 10 minutes, plus 4 to 8 hours to marinate | Cooking time: 18 to 20 minutes | Serves: 6 | Equipment: grill, kamado, or fire pit

4 to 5 pounds chicken legs (about 12 legs)

¼ cup extra virgin olive oil

¼ cup lemon juice

½ tablespoon coarse Kosher salt

½ teaspoon ground black pepper

4 tablespoons (about 1 bulb) minced garlic

10 thyme stems, leaves attached

1. Place chicken legs in a zip-top gallon bag and add remaining ingredients. Seal bag and shake to coat all the chicken.

2. Place the bag in the refrigerator for 4 to 8 hours, shaking and turning occasionally, if possible, to make sure all the chicken is evenly coated.

3. Prepare and light a grill, kamado, or fire pit with a cooking grate for two-zone cooking over medium heat, and oil the grate to prevent sticking.

4. Place marinated chicken legs on the grill. Cook over medium-high heat for 5 minutes per side, turning the legs 3 to 4 times, for a total of 18 to 20 minutes. Move legs to cooler section, as needed, to prevent burning and overcooking.

5. Remove from grill and let rest 5 minutes before serving.

Blackberry BBQ Chicken

Every summer, we drive an hour and half north of Phoenix to our secret place where wild blackberries grow. We pick as many as we can, and this is the first meal I make when we get home. So, when blackberries are in season or on sale at the grocery store, this barbecue chicken is a must.

Prep time: 15 minutes | *Cooking time:* 10 to 20 minutes | *Serves:* 4
| *Equipment:* grill, kamado, or fire pit

2 teaspoons coarse Kosher salt

½ teaspoon ground black pepper

1 teaspoon garlic powder

1½ to 2 pounds boneless, skinless chicken breasts

Blackberry BBQ Sauce (see below)

1. Prepare and light a grill, kamado, or fire pit with a cooking grate for direct cooking over high heat.

2. Combine salt, pepper, and garlic powder in a small bowl. Season chicken breasts on both sides with garlic-salt mixture.

3. Place on grill directly over the fire for 3 minutes. Flip chicken and baste with Blackberry BBQ Sauce. Cook for 3 more minutes.

4. Flip chicken breast again and baste other side with barbecue sauce. Let cook for 3 minutes. Flip one more time and cook for about 1 minute or until chicken is fully cooked, 10 to 20 minutes total.

Blackberry BBQ Sauce

6 ounces (1 to 1¼ cups) blackberries

¼ cup ketchup

¼ cup sugar

⅛ cup apple cider vinegar

2 tablespoons light brown sugar, packed

2 teaspoons hot sauce

2 cloves garlic, finely minced

1 teaspoon ground dry mustard

1 teaspoon fresh grated ginger

½ teaspoon ground black pepper

½ teaspoon coarse Kosher salt

1. Combine all the ingredients in a medium saucepan over medium-high heat for 10 minutes, stirring occasionally. Taste and adjust seasoning with additional sugar and/or salt and pepper. Blackberry BBQ Sauce will be very thick.

2. Pour into a glass jar, cover, and use immediately or refrigerate for up to 1 week.

Garlic Ranch Spatchcock Chicken

Don't let this chicken recipe scare you! Spatchcocking a chicken is so easy with a good pair of kitchen shears. The result is a whole chicken that cooks so fast that the juices are sealed in. The best part is the insanely crispy skin, my favorite part of a whole chicken. Make your own ranch mix for this chicken, it's so worth it. Plus, then you'll have extra to turn into dressing for a salad or even sprinkle on popcorn.

Prep time: *15 minutes* | **Cooking time:** *25 to 30 minutes* | **Serves:** *4* | **Equipment:** *pizza oven*

1 large (3- to 4-pound) roaster chicken, neck and other organs removed

1 (24-ounce) package small new potatoes, cut into large chunks

2 tablespoons extra virgin olive oil

1 teaspoon coarse Kosher salt

4 tablespoons butter, softened

3 tablespoons (or 1 packet) dry ranch mix (recipe follows)

8 to 10 cloves garlic

1. Prepare a wood-fired pizza oven with a 500°F fire that's been burning for about an hour.

2. Pat chicken dry. Place the chicken breast-side down, use poultry shears to cut along each side of the chicken's backbone, and remove it. Turn chicken breast-side up and press on the breastbone to flatten chicken.

3. Toss new potatoes with olive oil and salt, then set aside.

4. In a small bowl, combine butter and ranch mix. Rub mixture all over both sides of the chicken, including under the skin.

5. Transfer chicken to a large 18 x13-inch baking sheet covered with tinfoil with the skin-side up, and tuck garlic cloves underneath the chicken. Add potatoes around the sides of the chicken.

6. Place in your wood-fired oven for 25 to 30 minutes, turning every 10 to 15 minutes until the skin is browned and crispy and internal temperature is 165°F (insert thermometer into the thickest part of the thigh, but not touching bone, to read temperature of a whole bird).

7. Remove from wood-fired oven, allow to cool, carve, and serve with a fresh salad.

Ranch Mix

⅓ cup dry powdered buttermilk

2 tablespoons dried parsley

2 teaspoons garlic powder

2 teaspoons onion powder

2 teaspoons dried onion flakes

1½ teaspoons dried dill weed

1 teaspoon ground black pepper

1 teaspoon dried chives

1 teaspoon coarse Kosher salt

In a medium bowl, whisk all ingredients together until blended. Store in a sealed container in the refrigerator for up to 3 months.

NOTE: Three tablespoons of this mix equals 1 packet of the store-bought seasoning mix. To make ranch dressing, combine 1 tablespoon seasoning mix with ⅓ cup mayo or Greek yogurt and ⅓ cup milk, and whisk to combine.

Herbes de Provence Rotisserie Chicken

My husband travels a lot and I always ask him to bring home herbs, seasonings, and cookbooks from his travels. Earlier this year he happened to be in the Provence region of France and brought home a big bag of herbes de Provence. Herbes de Provence can also be found at your local grocery store, or you can even make your own blend.

Prep time: 10 minutes | Cooking time: 60 to 70 minutes | Serves: 4 | Equipment: rotisserie grill

2 tablespoons extra virgin olive oil

2 tablespoons dried herbes de Provence

1 tablespoon coarse Kosher salt

2 (3½-pound) chickens

1. Prep the grill for the rotisserie, removing grates if you need to and placing a piece of tinfoil or a small tinfoil pan in the middle to catch the drippings.

2. Prepare a medium-high indirect fire with fire on both sides of where the chicken will be. Plan to replenish the wood every 20 minutes or so during the cooking time to keep the fire hot (or use all lump charcoal for a longer-lasting heat source).

3. In a small bowl, combine olive oil, herbes de Provence, and salt. Rub mixture all over the outside of the chicken and in the cavity, including under the skin.

4. Follow grill instructions to place both chickens securely on the spit, using butcher's twine if necessary.

5. Turn on the rotisserie and grill over indirect heat with the lid closed for 60 to 70 minutes or until the skin is browned and crispy, with an internal temperature of 165°F (insert thermometer into the thickest part of the thigh, but not touching bone, to read temperature of a whole bird).

6. Slide chicken off spit and onto platter. Let the meat rest under a tinfoil tent for 8 to 10 minutes before carving.

NOTE: Plan for 20 to 30 minutes per pound to cook a chicken at a cooking temperature between 300 and 350°F.

BBQ Chicken Pizza

Skip the cheese and pepperoni because this BBQ Chicken Pizza might just become your newest favorite. This is a great way to use up leftover chicken.

Prep time: 30 minutes | Cooking time: 2 minutes | Serves: 4
| Equipment: pizza oven

1 recipe Classic Pizza Dough (page 114)

4 tablespoons extra virgin olive oil

2 cups shredded, cooked chicken

8 slices cooked bacon, crumbled

½ cup blue cheese crumbles

2 green onions, chopped

1 cup shredded mozzarella cheese

½ cup barbecue sauce

1. Prepare a wood-fired pizza oven with a 700 to 800°F fire that's been burning for about an hour.

2. Roll out pizza dough on a pizza peel that is lightly floured and dusted with corn meal.

Brush with olive oil and then top with one-quarter of the cooked chicken, bacon, blue cheese, green onions, and a little mozzarella cheese. Then drizzle a little barbecue sauce over the pizza. Repeat with remaining dough and toppings.

3. Make sure the dough isn't sticking to the pizza peel. Gently place in the pizza oven by sliding it off the pizza peel. Cook for 1 minute, rotate, and cook for an additional minute or until crust reaches desired consistency and cheese is melted.

NOTE: If you are cooking in a kamado, use indirect heat with a pizza stone on the cooking grid. It is very important to let the stone and ceramics of the kamado grill preheat to 500°F for 45 minutes to get a full "pizza oven" effect. The air temperature will reach 500°F quickly but it takes time for the ceramics to heat up all the way.

Slide pizza off the peel onto the stone and cook until the toppings brown slightly and the crust is nicely browned, 5 to 15 minutes depending on the toppings, crust, and cook temperature.

Rotisserie Cajun Turkey

Don't let your next Thanksgiving turkey be dry and boring. Set up a rotisserie with indirect heat and let this flavorful holiday bird baste itself on the grill while you use the oven for all the sides.

Prep time: 20 minutes, plus 1 hour standing time | Cooking time: 4 to 5 hours | Serves: 4 | Equipment: rotisserie grill

1 (12- to 14-pound) turkey

1 to 1½ cups Cajun Seasoning (page 24)

½ cup butter (1 stick), softened

1. Prepare the grill for the rotisserie, removing grates if you need to and placing a piece of tinfoil or a small tinfoil pan in the middle to catch the drippings.

2. Remove turkey from refrigerator; let stand at room temperature for 1 hour.

3. Prepare a medium-high indirect fire with fire on both sides of where the turkey will be. Plan to replenish the wood every 20 minutes or so during the cooking time to keep the fire hot (or use all lump charcoal for a longer-lasting heat source).

4. Meanwhile, combine Cajun seasoning and softened butter in a small bowl.

5. Pat turkey dry with paper towels. Rub Cajun butter all over the turkey and inside the cavity as well.

6. Place turkey on rotisserie and tie legs and wings of turkey close to the body to prevent them from dragging on the grill. Turn the turkey on the rotisserie and watch turkey for a few minutes, adjusting counter balance so the turkey turns smoothly. Place a drip pan with a cup of water under the bird to catch any drippings (use drippings to make gravy).

7. Check on turkey every 45 minutes or so and add more lump charcoal and wood as needed to maintain optimal cooking temperature.

8. Check for doneness in several areas and avoid touching the spit or bone with thermometer. A whole turkey is done at 165°F in the innermost part of the thigh and wing and the thickest part of the breast.

9. Remove from rotisserie and let cool slightly before removing the spit. Serve warm.

NOTE: The cooking time is 15 to 20 minutes per pound, so a 12-pound turkey will take 4 hours and a 15-pound turkey will take 5 hours. Cooking anything larger than a 15-pound turkey on a rotisserie can be troublesome. Rotisseries can't handle the weight and a lot of grills, especially gas grills, simply aren't large enough for that size turkey.

To balance the turkey, place the rotisserie rod with the turkey on the grill so that it moves freely. The heavy side of the turkey will drop toward the bottom of the grill. Pull the counterbalance straight up and tighten. It won't balance perfectly, but it will offset the weight enough to allow the rotisserie motor to handle the heavy load easier.

Grilled Teriyaki Shrimp Kabobs

These shrimp skewers make a great appetizer or light supper on a hot summer day.

Prep time: 30 minutes, plus 15 minutes to marinate | Cooking time: 5 minutes | Serves: 4 | Equipment: grill, kamado, or fire pit

6 bamboo skewers

1½ cups water

¾ cup brown sugar, packed

½ cup low-sodium soy sauce

3 tablespoons cornstarch

1½ teaspoons garlic powder

1 teaspoon sesame oil

1 teaspoon mirin (sweet rice wine)

1 pound raw jumbo shrimp, peeled and deveined (about 25 shrimp)

½ cup chopped cilantro, to serve

1 tablespoon sesame seeds, to serve

1. Prepare and light a grill, kamado, or fire pit with a cooking grate for direct cooking over medium-high heat.

2. Soak bamboo skewers in water while prepping the recipe.

3. In a medium saucepan, combine water, brown sugar, soy sauce, cornstarch, garlic powder, sesame oil, and mirin, and stir to combine. Stir over medium heat until thickened, about 10 minutes, then remove from heat and set aside.

4. Add half of the sauce and the shrimp to a zip-top gallon bag, seal, and marinate for 15 minutes.

5. Thread shrimp on skewers and discard the marinade. Cook shrimp on a preheated grill over medium heat, flipping halfway through, cooking until shrimp is pink and cooked through, about 5 minutes.

6. Serve shrimp immediately with remaining sauce. Sprinkle with chopped cilantro and sesame seeds.

Cedar Plank Dill Salmon

Adding dill in the seasoning blend and making a compound butter with fresh dill really adds a ton of flavor to salmon. And not only does using soaked cedar planks add flavor to the fish, it protects it from harsh flames during the cooking process. Change it up by using different types of wood planks; there are several varieties available at grocery stores and online, but make sure to buy wood suitable for cooking food. Alder is another great option!

Prep time: *20 minutes, plus 1 hour to soak* | **Cooking time:** *12 to 15 minutes* | **Serves:** *4* | **Equipment:** *grill, kamado, or fire pit*

2 cedar planks, for grilling

½ teaspoon coarse Kosher salt

½ teaspoon garlic powder

½ teaspoon dried dill weed

¼ teaspoon ground black pepper

4 pieces (about 1¼ pounds) salmon

4 tablespoons Dill Butter (see below), sliced in 1-tablespoon pieces

1. Soak cedar planks for 1 hour before grilling.

2. Prepare and light a grill, kamado, or fire pit with a cooking grate for direct cooking over medium-high heat.

3. Combine salt, garlic, dill, and pepper in a small bowl.

4. Season salmon with dill seasoning and place 2 pieces of salmon on each cedar plank.

Place planks over direct heat and cook for 12 to 15 minutes, or until salmon is opaque and flaky, with a temperature of 145°F in the thickest part of the salmon.

5. Add a pat of Dill Butter to each piece of salmon during the last minute of cooking. Serve warm.

NOTE: The cedar plank may catch fire while cooking, so keep the flames down with a squirt of water from a water bottle.

Dill Butter

4 tablespoons butter, softened

2 tablespoons chopped fresh dill

1 teaspoon minced garlic

Combine all ingredients in a medium bowl. Spoon mixture out onto a piece of plastic wrap and gently roll up to create a log shape of dill butter. Place in refrigerator for 2 hours or overnight to harden.

Sweet Chili Halibut with Mango Salsa

When mangoes are in season, this recipe needs to be on the top of your list. It's like a taste of summer in the Caribbean. Serve with Coconut Rice (see recipe below) to really add to the summer beach vibe.

Prep time: 30 minutes | *Cooking time:* 10 minutes | *Serves:* 4 | *Equipment:* grill, kamado, or fire pit

MANGO SALSA

2 medium firm, ripe mangoes, diced small

1 large shallot, finely minced

1 small (or ½ large) jalapeño, seeded and finely minced

2 tablespoons fresh lime juice

2 tablespoons finely chopped cilantro

1 teaspoon coarse Kosher salt

¼ teaspoon ground black pepper

HALIBUT

3 tablespoons sugar

1 tablespoon ground chili powder

½ teaspoon coarse Kosher salt

4 (6-ounce) halibut fillets

1. Prepare and light a grill, kamado, or fire pit with a cooking grate for direct cooking over medium-high heat.

2. While the grill heats up, prepare the Mango Salsa. In a medium bowl, mix together the mango, shallot, jalapeño, lime juice, cilantro, salt, and pepper, and store in the fridge until ready to use.

3. Make a spice rub by combining sugar, chili powder, and salt in a small bowl.

4. Rub the spice mixture on one side of the halibut fillets. Place halibut on grill and cook for 4 to 5 minutes per side. Halibut should be firm but give a little when done.

5. Serve halibut topped with Mango Salsa and Coconut Rice, if desired.

Coconut Rice

1½ cups coconut water

1¼ cups canned coconut milk

1½ cups jasmine rice, rinsed and drained well

½ teaspoon coarse Kosher salt

In a medium saucepan, bring coconut water, coconut milk, rice, and salt to a full boil. Cover and simmer until liquid has been absorbed, about 20 minutes. Fluff with a fork, then let rest 5 minutes.

Blackened Salmon

Simple blackened salmon is our go-to salmon recipe. It has so much flavor and is ready start to finish in under 30 minutes. Serve with grilled asparagus, rice, and a green salad.

Prep time: *10 minutes* | **Cooking time:** *10 to 20 minutes* | **Serves:** *4* | **Equipment:** *grill, kamado, or fire pit*

1 tablespoon paprika

1 tablespoon sugar

2 teaspoons coarse Kosher salt

2 teaspoons ground black pepper

1 teaspoon garlic powder

1 teaspoon onion powder

½ teaspoon dried thyme

½ teaspoon dried oregano

½ teaspoon ground cumin

¼ teaspoon cayenne pepper

1 (1¼-pound) salmon fillet

1. Prepare and light a grill, kamado, or fire pit with a cooking grate for direct cooking over medium-high heat.

2. Combine spices in an airtight container. Generously sprinkle salmon with seasoning (you won't use all the seasoning that you made).

3. Oil grill and place salmon on grill using indirect heat (3 to 4 inches away from heat). Grill fillet for 4 to 6 minutes (2 to 3 minutes per side) per ½ inch thickness, turning only once.

4. Cook salmon until the meat begins to change color and becomes flaky and then check for doneness by inserting the tip of a sharp knife near the thickest part of the salmon and pull slightly. Well-done salmon appears opaque and will flake easily.

NOTE: Salmon continues to cook after being removed from the grill.

Grilled Cheese Sandwiches

In my house, we call these "grown-up grilled cheeses." Not only are they actually grilled, but the combination of cheeses and the addition of sliced tomato really transforms a childhood favorite into a delicious comfort food meal.

Prep time: *10 minutes* | **Cooking time:** *8 to 10 minutes* | **Serves:** *6* | **Equipment:** *grill, kamado, or fire pit*

1 round (1-pound) sourdough loaf, cut into at least 12 slices

6 tablespoons salted butter, softened

6 tablespoons mayonnaise

12 slices Colby Jack cheese

12 slices pepper Jack cheese

2 large tomatoes, cut into 12 slices

½ cup grated Parmesan cheese

1. Prepare and light a grill, kamado, or fire pit with a cooking grate for direct cooking over medium heat.

2. Spread the outside of each slice of bread with butter.

3. On 1 slice of bread, spread with 1 tablespoon of mayonnaise.

4. Arrange two slices of Colby Jack and pepper Jack cheese on the side without mayonnaise. On the mayonnaise side, add 2 slices of tomato. Place the cheese and tomato sides together, ensuring the butter sides are facing outward.

5. Sprinkle the Parmesan over both buttered sides of the bread, pressing the cheese gently into the bread to adhere.

6. Repeat with remaining slices. Place the sandwiches on the grill and cook until golden on each side, 4 to 5 minutes per side.

NOTE: Try different cheese such as sharp cheddar, fontina, or Havarti.

5–Can Vegetarian Chili

This is one pot of chili that even the meateaters in the crowd will love! It's a great option for camping since no refrigeration is needed for the ingredients, and it's ready in 30 minutes.

Prep time: 5 minutes | Cooking time: 25 minutes | Serves: 4
| Equipment: grill, kamado, or fire pit

1 tablespoon extra virgin olive oil

1 medium onion, finely chopped

1 (14-ounce) can black beans, drained

1 (14-ounce) can red kidney beans, drained

1 (14-ounce) can diced tomatoes, with juice

1 (15-ounce) can tomato sauce

1 (4-ounce) can diced green chilies

2 tablespoons chili powder

2 teaspoons ground cumin

1 teaspoon garlic powder

1 teaspoon coarse Kosher salt

¾ teaspoon ground black pepper

1 cup water

cheese, green onions, avocado, crackers, and sour cream, to serve, optional

1. Prepare and light a grill, kamado, or fire pit with a cooking grate for direct cooking over medium heat.

2. In a large Dutch oven, heat the olive oil for 1 minute then add the onions. Sauté until onions begin to soften and turn translucent, about 5 minutes. Add remaining ingredients and stir to combine.

3. Cook chili about 20 minutes, stirring often. Serve immediately with your choice of toppings and cornbread on the side!

Grilled Portobello Mushroom Pizzas

You don't have to be vegetarian to enjoy these pizzas. Make sure to take the time to clean the mushrooms well so no dirt ends up in the pizzas.

Prep time: *15 minutes* | ***Cooking time:*** *10 to 15 minutes* | ***Serves:*** *2* | ***Equipment:*** *grill, kamado, or fire pit*

4 large Portobello mushrooms

¼ teaspoon garlic powder

¼ teaspoon ground black pepper

½ cup marinara or pizza sauce

1 cup shredded mozzarella cheese

peppers, onion, black olives, basil, tomato, garlic, to top

1. Prepare and light a grill, kamado, or fire pit with a cooking grate for direct cooking over medium heat with a pizza stone that's been preheated for at least 30 minutes.

2. Wipe the outside of the mushrooms with a damp paper towel, cut off the stems, and gently scrape out the gills.

3. Place the mushrooms top-side down on a cutting board. Sprinkle each mushroom with a pinch of garlic powder and a quick grind of pepper.

4. Top mushrooms with marinara or pizza sauce, mozzarella cheese, and desired toppings.

5. Transfer prepared mushrooms to preheated baking stone on the grill. Grill for 10 to 15 minutes or until mushrooms are cooked through, toppings are tender, and cheese is bubbly. Serve immediately.

Baked Spinach & 3 Cheese Rigatoni

Talk about comfort food! This rigatoni is perfect for a cold night, cuddling on the couch with your sweetie or a good ol' big family supper! Try adding chopped red bell peppers for even more flavor. Serve with green salad and garlic bread.

Prep time: 15 minutes | Cooking time: 23 minutes | Serves: 6 to 8 | Equipment: pizza oven

1 (16-ounce) package rigatoni pasta

24 ounces ricotta cheese

1 pound shredded mozzarella cheese

1 egg, beaten

1½ cups spaghetti sauce (homemade or store-bought)

1 (6-ounce) bag (about 4 cups) baby spinach

2 tablespoons minced garlic

2 teaspoons salt

¼ teaspoon red pepper flakes

½ cup grated Parmesan cheese

1. Prepare a wood-fired pizza oven with a 400 to 425°F fire that's been burning for about an hour (or use residual heat in the oven from a previous fire).

2. Bring a large pot of lightly salted water to a boil. Add rigatoni and cook for 8 minutes, which is slightly undercooked, then drain. Return rigatoni to cooking pot.

3. In a large bowl, mix ricotta cheese, mozzarella cheese, egg, spaghetti sauce, spinach, garlic, salt, and red pepper. Add ricotta mixture to the cooking pot and stir well combine.

4. Spray a 9 x 13-inch baking dish with nonstick cooking spray and spoon in rigatoni mixture. Top with Parmesan cheese.

5. Bake in preheated pizza oven for 15 minutes, turning halfway through cooking time. Let stand for 15 minutes before serving.

Vegetable Kabobs with Mustard BBQ Sauce

Meat-eating friends won't miss the meat when these vegetable kabobs hit their plates. Try changing up the vegetables by using what's in season.

Prep time: 30 minutes, plus 60 minutes to soak | *Cooking time:* 28 minutes | *Serves:* 4 | *Equipment:* grill, kamado, or fire pit

MUSTARD BBQ SAUCE

¾ cup yellow mustard

¾ cup apple cider vinegar

2 tablespoons light brown sugar, packed

1½ tablespoons butter (regular or dairy free)

1 tablespoon ketchup

1 teaspoon coarse Kosher salt

½ teaspoon ground black pepper

1 teaspoon hot sauce (like Frank's)

1 teaspoon garlic powder

KEBABS

4 medium zucchinis, cut into 2-inch pieces

4 bell peppers, any color, cut into 2-inch pieces

2 large red onions, cut into 2-inch pieces

1 (8-ounce) container whole button mushrooms

1 (10-ounce) container grape or cherry tomatoes

10 small potatoes

10 bamboo skewers

1. Soak bamboo skewers in water for 60 minutes.

2. In a medium saucepan, combine all the ingredients for the barbecue sauce, stir, and let simmer over medium-low heat for 10 minutes, stirring occasionally.

3. Prepare and light a grill, kamado, or fire pit with a cooking grate for direct cooking over medium-high heat.

4. Remove bamboo skewers from water and fill up skewers with various vegetables. Leave a 2-inch piece of bamboo open at the end for easy turning and top the skewers with a potato or a mushroom to help keep everything secure.

5. Remove barbecue sauce from heat, taste, and adjust seasonings. Reserve half the sauce.

6. Place skewers on the grill over direct heat for 6 minutes. Turn and let cook 6 more minutes.

7. Turn once again and baste with barbecue sauce. Let cook 3 minutes before turning again. Baste and let finish cooking, about 3 more minutes.

8. Let cool slightly before serving with reserved Mustard BBQ Sauce.

SIDES

Grilled Mexican Corn

Sweet grilled corn topped with a creamy, spicy sauce is what summer is all about. This is a great addition to a big, juicy steak or just an afternoon snack. Can't find Cotija cheese? Try Parmesan or feta.

Prep time: *30 minutes, plus 30 minutes to soak* | **Cooking time:** *30 minutes* | **Serves:** *4* | **Equipment:** *grill, kamado, or fire pit*

4 ears corn, husks pulled down and silk removed

2 tablespoons plus 1 teaspoon coarse Kosher salt, divided

4 tablespoons low-fat mayonnaise

4 tablespoons nonfat plain yogurt

2 teaspoons paprika

1 teaspoon chili powder

4 to 6 tablespoons crumbled Cotija cheese

1 lime, cut into 4 wedges

1. Soak corn in a 6-quart stockpot filled with about 5 quarts water and 2 tablespoons coarse Kosher salt for 30 minutes.

2. Meanwhile, prepare and light a grill, kamado, or fire pit with a cooking grate for direct cooking over medium-high heat.

3. Combine mayonnaise, yogurt, paprika, chili powder, and remaining 1 teaspoon salt in a small bowl. Set aside.

4. Grill corn, turning occasionally, until marked and tender, about 30 minutes total. Spread each ear with 1 tablespoon of the sauce and sprinkle with 1 tablespoon Cotija cheese. Serve with lime wedges.

NOTE: Keep the husks away from direct fire if possible as they will catch fire easily. Try hanging the husks off the edge of the grill (away from the fire) and keeping the fire directly under the corn.

Grilled Ratatouille

This hearty, seasonal side dish takes on a delicious flavor over the fire. Serve alongside chicken or fish, or mix into pasta or over rice for a meatless meal.

Prep time: 30 minutes | *Cooking time:* 12 minutes | *Serves:* 4
| *Equipment:* grill, kamado, or fire pit

2 zucchinis, cut into 1-inch pieces

2 yellow squash, cut into 1-inch pieces

2 eggplants, cut into 1-inch pieces

2 red bell peppers, cut into 1-inch pieces

2 red onions, cut into 1-inch pieces

1 pint cherry tomatoes

½ cup plus 2 tablespoons extra virgin olive oil

3 tablespoons (about 1 bulb) minced garlic

½ tablespoon dried Italian herb blend

½ tablespoon coarse Kosher salt

1. Prepare and light a grill, kamado, or fire pit with a cooking grate for direct cooking over medium-high heat.

2. Place all cut vegetables and tomatoes in a 9 x 13-inch disposable tin pan.

3. Add olive oil, garlic, Italian seasoning, and salt, and toss to coat.

4. Place pan on the grill and cook for 12 minutes, turning and stirring every 3 minutes through the cooking time. Serve at room temperature.

Roasted Garlic Broccoli

Broccoli is one of the easiest vegetables to cook on the grill. We have it twice a week all year long and pretty much this is the only way I serve it, with just a little olive oil, salt, and garlic. It's the perfect side dish for steaks, burgers, chicken, and really any other protein. Frozen broccoli also works in this recipe—just thaw it fully before grilling.

Prep time: 5 minutes | Cooking time: 10 minutes | Serves: 4
| Equipment: grill, kamado, or fire pit

1 head broccoli, chopped into bite-sized pieces

12 cloves of garlic, divided

2 tablespoons extra virgin olive oil

½ tablespoon coarse Kosher salt

1. Prepare and light a grill, kamado, or fire pit with a cooking grate for indirect cooking over medium-high heat.

2. Place broccoli in a large grill basket.

3. Finely mince 4 cloves of garlic and leave the other 8 whole. Drizzle broccoli with olive oil and then add in all the garlic and salt. Toss gently to coat broccoli.

4. Grill broccoli using medium-hot indirect heat for 10 minutes or until the broccoli is cooked and tender. Broccoli should be green with a slight toasty-black color on the ends.

NOTE: This broccoli uses indirect cooking, so it's perfect to cook while you cook your main dish over direct heat. Just throw the broccoli on the side and it will be perfect.

Grilled Italian Vegetable Basket

These are the easiest grilled veggies! I make them all year long.

Prep time: *10 minutes, plus 4 to 6 hours to marinate* | ***Cooking time:*** *15 to 20 minutes* |
Serves: *4* | ***Equipment:*** *grill, kamado, or fire pit*

1 cup sugar snap peas

1 to 2 red bell peppers, cut into 1-inch pieces

1 large sweet onion, cut into 1-inch pieces

1 pint grape or cherry tomatoes

2 zucchinis, cut into 1-inch pieces

½ cup Italian Salad Dressing (see below)

coarse Kosher salt and ground black pepper

1. Place cut vegetables and Italian salad dressing into a zip-top gallon bag. Seal, then shake and squish bag well to coat all the vegetables. Place bag in the refrigerator to marinate vegetables for at least 4 to 6 hours.

2. Prepare and light a grill, kamado, or fire pit with a cooking grate for direct cooking over medium-high heat.

3. Drain vegetables into a colander placed in the sink and let excess dressing drain. Spray a grill basket with nonstick cooking spray and place drained vegetables in the basket in a single layer.

4. Cook 15 to 20 minutes with grill lid closed, stirring the vegetables every 5 minutes or so to ensure they get lightly browned on all sides. Cooked vegetables should be slightly crisp and starting to char on the edges.

5. Serve hot and season with coarse Kosher and fresh ground black pepper.

Italian Salad Dressing

6 tablespoons olive oil

2 tablespoons apple cider vinegar

1 teaspoon dried parsley flakes

1 tablespoon fresh lemon juice

2 cloves garlic, chopped

¼ teaspoon red pepper flakes

½ tablespoon Italian herb blend

¼ teaspoon sugar

pinch of coarse Kosher salt

Combine all ingredients in a mason jar, screw on the lid, shake, and serve. Store leftovers in mason jar in the refrigerator for up to 1 week.

Foiled Blue Cheese Potatoes

Foiled potatoes were a staple side dish in my house growing up, and I still make the plain version all the time to go with steak. But, if you're a blue cheese fan, you are going to flip over these blue cheese potatoes.

Prep time: *10 minutes |*
Cooking time: *40 to 60 minutes | **Serves:** 4 |*
Equipment: *grill, kamado, or fire pit*

4 (11 x 13-inch) pieces aluminum foil

4 large potatoes, peeled and cut into ½-inch pieces

4 tablespoons butter

4 tablespoons crumbled blue cheese

2 teaspoons coarse Kosher salt

1 teaspoon ground black pepper

1 teaspoon garlic powder

1. Prepare and light a grill, kamado, or fire pit with a cooking grate for two-zone cooking over medium-high heat.

2. Lay out 4 pieces of aluminum foil. On each piece add one chopped potato and one-quarter of the butter, blue cheese, salt, pepper, and garlic powder. Fold up foil into packets, making sure to seal all the edges well by rolling and crimping the foil.

3. Place packets on grill over direct heat and flip/rotate every 10 minutes for 40 to 60 minutes. Check potatoes after 40 minutes to determine how much longer they need. Potatoes should be soft when pierced with the tip of a knife and starting to brown on the edges. Watch closely so potatoes and cheese don't burn. Move to indirect heat if potatoes and cheese are starting to burn.

NOTE: Use prechopped breakfast potatoes for quicker prep and cooking. They cook up a little faster and are great for camping so there is less peeling and chopping.

BREADS

Simple White Bread

This recipe was passed down to me by my father-in-law, who always makes it in his bread machine. I adapted it for the pizza oven, and it's just as simple and delicious. It's pretty much failproof, and all the ingredients go into the mixing bowl together! It's also great to use a mixture of white and wheat flours for a heartier loaf.

Prep time: 1 hour 30 minutes | Cooking time: 30 minutes | Serves: 6 to 8 | Equipment: pizza oven

1 tablespoon instant yeast

3 cups unbleached all-purpose flour

1 tablespoon sugar

1 teaspoon coarse Kosher salt

¾ stick butter, softened

2 eggs

1 cup hot (not boiling) water

1. Prepare a wood-fired pizza oven with a 400°F fire that's been burning for about an hour (or use residual heat in the oven from a previous fire).

2. Combine all ingredients in the bowl of an electric stand mixer. Mix on medium-high speed for 7 to 10 minutes (or until the dough starts to pull away from the bowl) with a dough hook attachment. Scrape down sides occasionally. Let dough rise in bowl for 30 minutes.

3. Turn mixer back on to medium-high speed for 2 to 3 minutes.

4. Spray a 9 x 5-inch loaf pan and hands with nonstick cooking spray. Turn dough out onto hands and work into the shape of the pan. Place in pan and let rise for 45 minutes in a warm area.

5. Place in 400°F pizza oven for 30 minutes to bake. If the oven has an active fire, leave the door open; however, if using residual heat, put the oven door back on to trap the heat for cooking. Remove from oven and let cool for 30 minutes before removing from pan. Then continue cooling for another 1 to 1½ hours before serving.

NOTE: Cutting the bread before it's completely cooled will result in a gummy texture.

Classic Pizza Dough

This is the easiest pizza dough. It comes together quickly, it's easy to roll out, and the best part—it has great flavor. Try adding dried herbs to the dough for even more flavor. Or remove the garlic from the recipe to use in sweet recipes.

Prep time: *20 minutes | **Rise time:** 80 minutes | **Makes:** 2 (1-pound) dough balls*

2 tablespoons instant yeast

2 cups lukewarm water (90°F)

2 tablespoons sugar

½ cup vegetable, canola, or extra virgin olive oil

1 teaspoon coarse Kosher salt

4 tablespoons minced garlic

5½ to 6 cups unbleached all-purpose flour, divided

1. In the bowl of an electric mixer, dissolve yeast in water and add sugar. Wait a few minutes.

2. Add oil, salt, and garlic. Fit electric mixer with dough hook, turn on low, add in 3 cups flour, and mix for about 10 minutes on medium-low speed until the dough leaves the side of the mixer bowl.

3. Add remaining flour until the dough completely pulls away from the bowl and forms a ball, then turn up the speed to medium-high to knead dough until smooth. Remove dough hook and allow dough to rise in the bowl until doubled in size, about 1 hour.

4. Use fist to gently punch down the risen dough. Divide dough into desired portions and roll each portion out on a floured surface or parchment paper, then let rise for an additional 20 minutes before rolling out and using.

This makes 2 cookie sheet–sized pizza doughs, enough for 8 individual pizzas or 16 calzones.

Bacon Onion Focaccia

This easy focaccia bread requires no special mixer, just a wooden spoon and it's ready in under an hour and a half. It's a great side for a big juicy steak or roasted chicken, plus the possibilities are endless. This is my family's favorite because who doesn't love bacon?

Prep time: 30 minutes | Rise time: 30 minutes | Cooking time: 25 to 35 minutes | Serves: 12 | Equipment: pizza oven

1 tablespoon instant yeast

2 cups lukewarm water

4¾ cups unbleached all-purpose flour, divided

4 tablespoons extra virgin olive oil, divided

1 teaspoon dried sage

3 teaspoons coarse Kosher salt, divided

1 onion, thinly sliced

1 red pepper, thinly sliced

4 slices thick-cut bacon, chopped

1. Prepare a wood-fired pizza oven with a 400°F fire that's been burning for about an hour (or use residual heat in the oven from a previous fire).

2. In a large bowl, sprinkle yeast over warm water. Let stand until foamy, about 5 minutes. Add 2½ cups flour, 2 tablespoons oil, sage, and 2 teaspoons salt to the mixture, and stir with a wooden spoon until smooth.

3. Stir in remaining flour a little at a time until dough begins to pull away from the bowl (dough will be wet and sticky). Cover and let rise in a warm area until doubled in size, about 30 minutes.

4. Meanwhile, heat 1 tablespoon oil in a medium skillet. Add in sliced onion, pepper, and chopped bacon. Cook until onion is tender and bacon is fully cooked, 10 to 12 minutes.

5. Coat a large 15 x 10 x 1-inch baking sheet with cooking spray and gently spread dough on the pan. Brush dough with remaining oil. Dip fingers in cold water and gently press into dough to form indentations. Spread onion mixture on top and sprinkle with remaining salt.

6. Place in hot pizza oven and bake for 15 to 20 minutes, rotating every 5 minutes. Bread will sound hollow when tapped. Remove from oven and place on a wire rack to cool. Cut into 12 pieces for serving.

VARIATIONS

If you don't like the onion, pepper, and bacon combination, you can try these other topping suggestions:

Florentine: 1 (10-ounce) package frozen spinach, thawed and squeezed dry; 5 slices bacon, cooked and chopped; and 1½ cups shredded fontina cheese

Garlic basil: 2 tablespoons minced fresh garlic and ¼ cup fresh basil leaves

Jalapeño cheddar: 1 to 2 fresh jalapeño peppers, finely sliced, and 1 cup shredded sharp cheddar cheese

Italian: ½ cup black pitted olives, halved; ½ cup sun-dried tomatoes in oil, roughly chopped; 1 to 2 tablespoons fresh rosemary leaves

Cast-Iron Buttermilk Biscuits

There is nothing better than hot fresh biscuits cooked over an open fire. The best part about these buttermilk biscuits is that there is no need to roll them out, just drop them by large spoonfuls into the pan. After the biscuits are finished, I take them out of the pan and whip up some cream gravy for a delicious campfire meal.

Prep time: *10 minutes* | **Cooking time:** *15 to 20 minutes* | **Serves:** *6 to 12* | **Equipment:** *grill, kamado, or fire pit*

2 cups unbleached all-purpose flour

1 tablespoon baking powder

½ teaspoon baking soda

2 teaspoons sugar

1 teaspoon coarse Kosher salt

1 cup cold buttermilk

½ cup (1 stick) butter, melted and cooled for about 5 minutes

1. Prepare and light a grill, kamado, or fire pit with a cooking grate for direct cooking over medium heat.

2. In a large bowl, whisk flour, baking powder, baking soda, sugar, and salt.

3. Combine buttermilk and cooled, melted butter in a medium bowl, stirring until thickened and slightly lumpy. Add buttermilk mixture to dry ingredients and stir until incorporated.

4. Using a greased ¼-cup dry measure (or two large spoons), scoop batter and drop onto a 12-inch cast-iron skillet. Repeat with remaining batter, spacing biscuits about 1½ inches apart.

5. Place cast-iron skillet over fire for 8 minutes and then rotate pan and continue cooking for an additional 7 to 10 minutes or until biscuits are lightly golden.

6. Cool slightly before serving.

Rustic Jalapeño Cheese Bread

This is the easiest bread and has such great flavor and texture. Cooking it without a pan gives it a rustic feel. I love taking this bread to potlucks and parties because it's so pretty and absolutely delicious.

Prep time: *30 minutes* | **Rise time:** *1 hour 15 minutes* | **Cooking time:** *30 minutes* | **Serves:** *6 to 8* | **Equipment:** *pizza oven*

1 tablespoon instant yeast

3 cups unbleached all-purpose flour

1 tablespoon sugar

1 teaspoon coarse Kosher salt

¾ stick butter, softened

2 eggs

1 cup hot (not boiling) water

2 cups shredded medium cheddar cheese

¼ cup pickled jalapeños, drained and patted dry

1. Prepare a wood-fired pizza oven with a 400°F fire that's been burning for about an hour (or use residual heat in the oven from a previous fire).

2. Combine first 7 ingredients in the bowl of an electric stand mixer. Mix on medium-high speed for 7 to 10 minutes (or until the dough starts to pull away from the bowl) with a dough hook attachment. Scrape down sides occasionally.

3. Remove bowl from mixer and stir in cheese and jalapeños with a wooden spoon. Let dough rise in bowl for 30 minutes at room temperature.

4. Place bowl back on the mixer and turn mixer back on to medium-high speed for 2 to 3 minutes. Sprinkle pizza peel with a little flour and set aside. Turn dough out onto hands and work dough into a ball shape, place on floured peel (making sure dough isn't sticking), and let rise for 45 minutes in a warm area.

5. Gently slide bread off the pizza peel in hot pizza oven for 30 minutes to bake. If the oven has an active fire leave the door open; however, if using residual heat put the oven door back on to trap the heat for cooking. Remove from oven and let cool for 1 to 1½ hours before serving.

NOTE: Cutting the bread before it's completely cooled will result in a gummy texture.

Grilled Garlic Parmesan Bread

Garlic bread is a staple in my house, but cooking it on the grill gives this simple side dish another level of flavor. It's easy to throw on one side of the grill while the rest of supper is cooking on the other side.

Prep time: 10 minutes | Cooking time: 6 minutes | Serves: 6 | Equipment: grill, kamado, or fire pit

½ cup extra virgin olive oil

½ teaspoon coarse Kosher salt

4 large garlic cloves, finely minced

¼ cup freshly grated Parmesan cheese

1 (16-ounce) loaf French bread, sliced into ¾-inch-thick slices

¼ cup chopped fresh parsley

1. Prepare and light a grill, kamado, or fire pit with a cooking grate for direct cooking over medium heat.

2. Add olive oil, salt, garlic, and Parmesan cheese to a shallow bowl. Stir to combine. Brush each slice of bread with the mixture, on both sides.

3. Grill bread for 1 to 3 minutes without turning, just until toasted. Flip bread over and toast for 1 to 3 minutes more.

4. Remove from grill and sprinkle with parsley and additional Parmesan cheese, if desired.

DESSERTS

Blueberry Cherry Crisp

I love making all sorts of fruit crisps for dessert—they're so easy to put together and adaptable to whatever fruit I have on hand. I took my favorite pie recipe and turned it into this easy crisp. Don't tell, but fruit crisps make a delicious breakfast too. They have fruit and oats, so that counts as breakfast!

Prep time: 15 minutes | *Cooking time:* 45 minutes | *Serves:* 6 to 8 | *Equipment:* grill, kamado, or fire pit

2 (6-ounce) containers fresh blueberries, rinsed and dried

1 (21-ounce) container cherry pie filling

¾ cup unbleached all-purpose flour

¾ cup rolled oats

1½ cups granulated sugar

½ cup (1 stick) butter, melted

1. Prepare and light a grill, kamado, or fire pit with a cooking grate for direct cooking over medium heat.

2. Combine berries and cherry pie filling in a medium bowl and pour into a 12-inch cast-iron skillet.

3. In another bowl, combine the flour, oats, sugar, and melted butter. Sprinkle the mixture over the fruit, making sure to completely cover them.

4. Place the skillet over direct heat for 45 minutes, turning occasionally. The crisp is done when the top is lightly browned and crisp.

5. Cool for 30 minutes before serving. Transfer any leftovers to a storage container, cover, and store in the refrigerator up to 1 week.

Peach Cobbler Dessert Pizza

Whenever we fire up the pizza oven, I make sure to have various items on hand for an end-of-the-night dessert pizza. This peach cobbler variety ended up becoming a family favorite.

Prep time: 15 minutes | Cooking time: 2 minutes | Serves: 8 | Equipment: pizza oven

1 recipe Sweet Dough (page 126)

2 tablespoons butter, melted

1 (21-ounce) can peach pie filling

1 cup powdered sugar

1 to 2 tablespoons milk

1. Prepare a wood-fired pizza oven with a 700 to 800°F fire that's been burning for about an hour.

2. Divide dough into 4 equal pieces and roll out each dough on a pizza peel that is lightly floured and dusted with corn meal. Brush with melted butter and then top each dough with one-quarter can of peach pie filling.

3. Make sure the dough isn't sticking to the pizza peel. Gently place in the pizza oven by sliding it off the pizza peel. Cook for 1 minute, rotate, and cook for an additional minute or until crust reaches desired consistency.

4. While pizza cools, combine powdered sugar and milk in a small bowl and drizzle over the pizza. Serve warm.

VARIATIONS:

Use any pie filling for a change. Top with powdered sugar glaze.

Mix ½ cup sugar with 2 tablespoons cinnamon for a cinnamon dessert pizza. Top with powdered sugar glaze.

Combine 8 ounces softened cream cheese, ⅓ cup sugar and ½ teaspoon vanilla, spread on cooked plain dough, and top with sliced fresh fruit with a drizzle of honey.

Coconut Rum Pineapple Rings

One of our local barbecue joints makes grilled pineapple rings as a side dish. It is amazing! But it was begging to be turned into a dessert, so I added some rum and coconut milk to add some richness, and it was perfect! Finish with a scoop of vanilla bean ice cream, whipped cream, and a drizzle of caramel syrup.

Prep time: 10 minutes | Cooking time: 8 to 12 minutes | Serves: 6 to 8 | Equipment: grill, kamado, or fire pit

1 (13.6-ounce) can coconut cream

½ cup coconut rum (or light rum)

1 cup light brown sugar, packed

1 pineapple, peeled, cored, and sliced

vanilla bean ice cream, whipped cream, and caramel syrup, to serve

1. Prepare and light a grill, kamado, or fire pit with a cooking grate for direct cooking over medium heat.

2. Combine coconut cream and rum in a shallow pie dish and mix well.

3. Place brown sugar in another shallow pie dish or plate. Dip both sides of the pineapple slice in the coconut rum mixture and then dip both sides into the brown sugar, and place on the grill over direct heat.

4. Grill for 4 to 6 minutes per side, or until pineapple is lightly golden and tender. Serve warm with a scoop of vanilla bean ice cream, whipped cream, and a drizzle of caramel syrup.

NOTE: Make sure to clean grill well after cooking these pineapple rings, otherwise ants will be attracted to the leftover sugar residue.

Chocolate Banana Calzones

These calzones are the perfect ending to any meal. They are great on the grill or in the pizza oven. The possibilities for these dessert calzones are endless.

Prep time: 30 minutes | Cooking time: 5 to 10 minutes | Serves: 16 | Equipment: pizza oven

1 recipe Sweet Dough (page 126)

4 bananas, each sliced into 4 pieces

3 to 4 cups chocolate chips

3 eggs, beaten

1 cup sugar

1. Prepare a wood-fired pizza oven with a 400 to 450°F fire that's been burning for about an hour (or use residual heat in the oven from a previous fire).

2. Roll out prepared dough into a thin, flat disc.

3. Add one-quarter of a banana and ¼ cup of chocolate chips to one side of the dough. Fold over the other side, creating a pocket for the filling. Pinch the edges closed and turn them under.

4. Cut three slits in the top, brush the top with beaten egg, and sprinkle heavily with sugar. Repeat with remaining dough and fillings.

5. Transfer to pizza oven and let cook for 5 to 10 minutes depending on the temperature of the oven, rotating halfway through cooking time. Calzones are done when they are lightly golden and chocolate is melted.

NOTE: These can be made in a kamado or grill that has a medium-heat fire for direct cooking with a pizza stone that's been preheated for at least 30 minutes. Temperature of the grill should be between 400 and 450°F. Calzones will take about 10 minutes to cook.

Sweet Dough

2 tablespoons instant yeast

2 cups lukewarm water (90°F)

2 tablespoons white sugar

½ cup vegetable or canola oil

1 teaspoon coarse Kosher salt

¼ cup brown sugar, packed

5½ to 6 cups unbleached all-purpose flour

1. Dissolve yeast in water and add white sugar in the bowl of an electric mixer, and wait a few minutes.

2. Add oil, salt, and brown sugar. Fit electric mixer with dough hook, turn on low, and mix in 3 cups flour. Mix for about 10 minutes on medium-low speed until the dough leaves the side of the mixer bowl.

3. Add remaining flour and turn up the speed to medium-high to knead dough until smooth. Remove dough hook and allow dough to rise in the bowl until doubled in size (about 1 hour).

4. Punch down. Divide dough into desired portions and roll each portion out on a floured surface or parchment paper, then let rise for an additional 20 minutes before rolling out and using.

This makes 2 cookie sheet–sized pizza doughs, enough for 8 individual pizzas or 16 calzones.